# LEICESTERSHIRE
# FOOD AND
# DRINK

D0188388

The History Press

First published 2009

The History Press
The Mill, Brimscombe Port
Stroud, Gloucestershire, GL5 2QG
www.thehistorypress.co.uk

© Rupert Matthews, 2009

The right of Rupert Matthews to be identified as the Author
of this work has been asserted in accordance with the
Copyrights, Designs and Patents Act 1988.

All rights reserved. No part of this book may be reprinted
or reproduced or utilised in any form or by any electronic,
mechanical or other means, now known or hereafter invented,
including photocopying and recording, or in any information
storage or retrieval system, without the permission in writing
from the Publishers.
British Library Cataloguing in Publication Data.
A catalogue record for this book is available from the British Library.

ISBN 978 0 7524 4863 3

Typesetting and origination by The History Press
Printed in Great Britain

# Contents

The church at Bottesford. The author was married in this beautiful church and lived in the village for a time after his marriage to a young woman from the village.

# FOREWORD

My wife was living in Bottesford in the Vale of Belvoir when we met. We were married there in the magnificent church that goes by the name of The Lady of the Vale of Belvoir, and our daughter was christened in the same place.

My wife introduced me to the delights of a Melton Mowbray pork pie on an early date while we were courting, and later showed me that there are two sorts of cheese known as Stilton – I had previously thought that there was only one. She has collected a number of recipes over the years and some of these are included in this book. I must also thank many other people who have helped with this book. It would be an impossible task to list them all, though you will find many of them listed as makers of fine foods and drinks at the back of this book. I must single out Angela Geary who has kindly allowed me access to her collection of old Leicestershire lore, including recipes and information on fruit varieties.

I have enjoyed researching this book, and must confess that my trousers are a touch tighter now than when I started.

Read, eat, drink, enjoy.

*Rupert Matthews*
*(May 2009)*

A pork pie as served in the home of the author's mother-in-law. It was when he was courting his future wife that the author was introduced to the fine foods of Leicestershire – and he has never looked back.

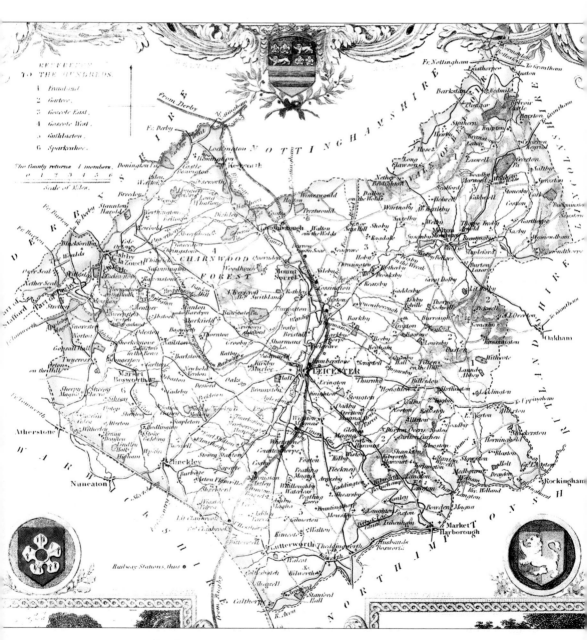

A map of Leicestershire printed in the 1850s. The city of Leicester is in the centre of the county, with the towns, villages, rivers, main roads and the first two railway lines clearly marked.

*One*

# LEICESTERSHIRE - THE COUNTY BEHIND THE FOOD

If there is one county in England which can boast of a culinary heritage of magnificent quality, wide variety and undoubted importance it is Leicestershire. Foods created here are recognised the world over, and consumed in quantities that defy the imagination. The names of small villages and market towns from this county are found on shop shelves in Australia, America, Canada and across Europe.

Melton Mowbray pork pies, Stilton cheese (both blue and white), Red Leicester cheese, Belvoir cake, Quorn puddings. All these and much more come from Leicestershire, but the county has far more to offer the dedicated foodie than these internationally known products.

The wide range of top quality foods to be found in Leicestershire is a tribute to the ingenuity and skills of the Leicestershire people, but it is founded on the county itself. The landscapes, soils and rocks of Leicestershire have been as instrumental in producing the county's foods and drinks as the people.

Most of Leicestershire is built on clay. The ground rises, swells and falls in a series of rolling hills that stretch to the horizon dotted by trees, topped by church spires and everywhere clothed in lush vegetation. The low lying, wetter grounds make for magnificent summer grazing for the cattle and sheep that form the basis of so many of the meat dishes of the county. Areas where the clay soil is better drained produce heavy crops of grain, potatoes and fruits or vegetables of all kinds. Mixed arable and livestock farming is typical of the county, producing a range of ingredients that has gone on to produce some classic dishes.

The keeping of pigs has long been characteristic of eastern Leicestershire where root vegetables and whey, a by-product of the dairy, have provided an ideal food source for pigs. The uses to which pork has been put by the good people of Leicestershire has been hailed as their greatest contribution to English cuisine. It is not only Melton Mowbray pork pies that have benefited from the large number of hogs kept in the area.

The rolling clay east of the county is divided from the more rugged west by the defining waterway of the county, the Soar. This river flows north through a broad, fertile valley until it empties into the Trent on the county's northern border near Nottingham. Most of the county drains into the Soar by way of streams such as the Rothley, Blackbrook, Fishpool and Wreak. These streams and rivers answer the one culinary demand that a landlocked county like Leicestershire might otherwise lack - fish. Without a coast there are no sea fish here, but the rivers and lakes of the county have traditionally been rich fishing grounds for a range of freshwater fish that have between them offered up some tasty and very tempting treats.

To the west of the Soar, the landscape is more broken than to the east and the clay soil less prevalent. In medieval times, Charnwood Forest was a deep and near impenetrable woodland covering some sixty square miles. It was characterised by craggy bluffs and tumbled boulders. These days much of the woodland has been cleared and the land improved for pasture. The trees still cling to the heights of Birch Hill, Cliffe Hill, Beacon and Bardon, all of which offer magnificent views over the county – even as far as Belvoir Castle on a clear day. It was on the cleared land that the Leicester sheep was developed, adding its own distinctive edge to the cuisine of the county.

Elsewhere in the west the landscape has been torn up for industrial purposes. Coal mining began 700 years ago in Coleorton, while in more recent centuries Coalville, Swannington, Ibstock and Bagworth have boomed and declined with the coal industry. But it is not only coal that is mined here. The Romans took granite from Mountsorrel and Groby to pave the mighty Fosse Way (now the A46 along much of its length) that cuts through the county from north-west to south-east on its way from Lincoln to Exeter. The Victorians came back for the self same granite. More recently the gravel beds of the north-west of the county have been exploited to manufacture concrete used to build motorways across England, and buildings as diverse as sewerage pumping stations and Olympic stadiums.

The great city of Leicester sits at the heart of the county, the centre occupying the same site it has done since the Romans built their city of Ratae Corieltauvorum here in AD 50 on

the site of an earlier Celtic town. The city formed the administrative centre for the county and adjacent areas in Roman times, and has dominated the economy of that same stretch of countryside ever since. In 1937 the League of Nations produced a report that named Leicester as the best city to live in to be found in the British Empire. Though the Empire has gone, the city remains an attractive place that has boomed in population as more and more people have moved to live here. What were once separate villages such as Knighton, Aylestone and Oadby have been brought into the city as suburbs.

The growing populations of the towns and city have provided a ready market for the foods and drinks produced by the rural areas. This has encouraged the production

A Melton Mowbray Pork Pie served with Stilton cheese – the classic combination of great Leicestershire foods.

A beer pump dispensing Everard's Tiger Bitter at a drinks festival. Tiger is one of the most popular beers produced by Everard's, itself the most popular brewery in the county.

of numerous delicacies and staples on a scale that would have been impossible without the urban demand. And the towns and cities have produced impressive products of their own. Most breweries have been, and still are, located in the towns, while bakeries and other processing units have turned out some great foods.

In recent decades the influx of people with cultural roots in the Indian subcontinent has brought an entirely new culinary tradition to the county. Today the Asian community in Leicester turns out a wide range of craft foods that can match in quality and variety the more traditionally English heritage of the county.

*Two*

# A HISTORY OF FOOD IN LEICESTERSHIRE

The delicious range of foods and drinks to be found in Leicestershire did not suddenly spring into being fully formed. They are the result of generations of experiments in cooking, farming and food production that has seen successes and failures with every passing century. People have lived in the area that was to become Leicester for at least 10,000 years – perhaps longer.

Mammoth steaks were on the earliest menus in Leicestershire, along with grilled aurochs and roasted wild boar. Such hearty meals have long gone, but they have been replaced by new ingredients and more refined cooking methods to produce the delights of today. It has been a long process, one shaped by violence and hardship as much as by the years of plenty and the cooking skills of the people.

When humans first came here, Britain was still joined to the continent of Europe by a land bridge of vast extent. The Soar and Trent emptied not into the North Sea via the Humber Estuary but onto a broad plain that stretched to Germany. The sea did not come in to make Britain an island until around 4,000 BC, by which time a well-established culture of hunting game and gathering wild plant foods was well established. The people of Leicestershire were part of a nomadic culture that stretched across northern Europe.

Fishing was a well established part of life with delicate fish hooks being carved out of bone and ivory and attached to lines. Fishing baskets of woven twigs served as effective nets, catching eels, trout and salmon as they did successfully almost into living memory. When a glut of fish was caught the flesh might be smoked to preserve it for a few days, but the nomads had no way of storing food and so they tended to gorge themselves, then rest up for a few days. Similar bouts of feasting affected the hunting of game animals. By around 5,000 BC the people in what is now Leicestershire were killing and eating deer, boar, hare and beaver as well as a number of birds such as duck, heron, grebe and swan. The fruit and vegetables eaten by these nomadic folk included blackberries, sloes, crab apples, dewberries, elderberries, nettles and wild celery.

Cooking methods at this date were simple in the extreme. Camp fires were made of wood, and any foods that were not eaten raw had to be cooked by fire. Meats were roasted or grilled over the flames, or they were slapped down on stones next to the fire for a gentler, more prolonged roasting. Some cuts might be placed into a deep pit in the ground, then covered with stone heated in a fire and covered over with leaves and then earth. This produced a longer, slower

A fishing scene from the Neolithic Age as imagined by a Victorian artist. The earliest farmers in Leicestershire continued to take wild foods whenever the opportunity presented itself, and the rivers of the county have always been rich in fish.

cooking method more suitable for tougher cuts when the preservation of moisture within the meat was essential.

The coming of agriculture produced not only a great increase in the types of ingredient available but also in cooking methods. Exactly when the farming way of life reached Leicestershire is unclear, but certainly there were farmers here by about 3500 BC. Archaeologists call this early British farming culture the Neolithic, meaning the New Stone Age. It was new because farming techniques were involved, but tools were still made of stone.

Because farmers raised crops in fields, they stayed put in one place from one year's end to the next. Unlike the nomads who had preceded them, the Neolithic farmers could afford to spend time building permanent homes. This in turn meant that they could make and own objects that would have been too large and heavy to carry about in a nomadic lifestyle. The earliest farmers introduced to Leicestershire were thus able to produce and use two key items of cooking equipment - the pottery pot and the oven.

The pottery pot, especially if manufactured with a lid, made possible boiling and stewing. For the first time food could be cooked in water. This by itself made it possible to eat tougher and harder foodstuffs than before, but also made it possible to mix together ingredients to produce entirely new dishes. Think of all those stews, casseroles and soups that we take for granted these days. Without a stew pot none of them would have been possible. When the metal pot came into use around 1000 BC it made possible frying at high temperatures for the first time.

The oven was no less revolutionary. It came to Britain rather later, perhaps around 800 BC. Unlike an open fire, it is relatively easy to control the temperature of an oven made of thick clay walls and fired by wood. Foods can be baked at high temperatures or low temperatures. They can be put in a cooling oven for slow cooking. They can be flash-fired at higher temperatures. Food would be surrounded by even cooking temperatures, not subjected to intense heat from one side only as was the case with a cooking fire. This made possible all sorts of baked goods. Cakes, bread, buns and other products of the bakery would be impossible without an oven.

The key crop of farming in Neolithic times was grain, namely wheat and barley. These two grains, later to be supplemented by rye, oats and others, allowed the early farmers to produce three types of food that have remained staples ever since: bread, pottage and beer. All three of these were heavily influenced by the fact that the early farmers had no weedkillers. All grain harvested was mixed with assorted weed seeds that added various types of flavour and nutrition, not all of them welcome, to the grains.

Pottage is today best known in the form of porridge, but in prehistoric times it came in a wide variety of forms. So far as can be deduced, pottages were produced by throwing into a pot rolled or cracked grains, water and whatever other foods were to hand. Small quantities of meat and vegetables were used to flavour the basic mix and ensured that everyone got a fair share of a scarce food item. Even fruits were added to pottage to make a sweet dish. Pottage would remain a food in Leicestershire among poorer folk well into the eighteenth century.

Bread was at first produced by mixing grain ground to flour with water and shaping the resulting paste into flat, round cakes. The paste was sometimes mixed with fat or honey to make them softer to eat. At first they were baked on hot stones beside the fire and probably ended up looking more like biscuits than bread. Once the oven was to hand, bread could be baked more evenly and would have been both easier to make and more pleasant to eat. When yeast was added to the mix, from around 500 BC onward, the first risen bread could be baked. Suddenly bread was much more enjoyable to eat than pottage. It rapidly overtook pottage as the most important way to cook grain crops.

The production of beer was as early as pottage, but is rather more controversial among historians. Nobody is entirely certain whether grain crops were consumed first in the form of pottage or as beer. Some believe that it was the attractions of alcoholic beer that persuaded nomadic hunter-gatherers to settle down to farm fields and build houses. Only then could they produce the heavy, bulky items needed to ferment beer. Seeing the earliest farmers as a bunch of boozy party-goers is an attractive image, but most historians think that it was the food benefits of grain that first made humans into farmers and that beer came later.

Be that as it may, beer brewing – both from barley and wheat – was known by the time farming reached Britain. The earliest of the famous Leicester ales no doubt came out of small scale cottage breweries sometime around 2,000 BC. The robust farmers of the county have not stopped drinking the stuff since.

By the time farming reached Britain, there was also a set collection of livestock. The animals kept by the early farmers had nothing to do with the game beasts the filled the woods and landscapes of prehistoric Britain. They would continue to be hunted for food down to the present day, but made no real contribution to farm livestock. The animals kept by the early farmers in Britain were descended from animals domesticated much earlier in the history of farming. These were animals which had temperaments which made them much more amenable to being kept by humans than did deer – or indeed woolly mammoths.

Sheep and goats came from the Middle East, where they were being herded by humans as early as 9000 BC. Cattle seem to have been domesticated in the Balkans by around 6000 BC. Pigs also came from southern Europe and seem to have been kept by humans by about 5000 BC, though this date is far from certain. The last of the domestic animals to reach Britain in prehistoric times was the chicken. This bird was descended from the red jungle fowl of northern India which was tamed around 4000 BC. The practice of keeping these productive birds spread both east and west from India, reaching Britain around 300 BC or perhaps a little later. The practice of keeping domestic ducks seems to have started only after the chicken arrived in Britain.

Sometime around 200 BC, vast salt pans were constructed on the Lincolnshire coast where salt was evaporated out of sea water in huge quantities. This was clearly far too much salt than was needed locally for cooking. Many people think that the massive surge in demand for salt was caused by the invention of methods of curing meat and fish for storage. Certainly herring were being smoked into kippers on the coast by this time but it is thought that salted fish was also being produced and shipped up the rivers to Leicestershire and overseas. Pork was probably being cured into ham and bacon at about this time. Perhaps the salt was itself moved up the Trent and Soar to allow the swineherds of Leicestershire to make bacon and ham.

The Romans came to Leicestershire in AD 47. The local tribe, the Coritani, seems to have been less hostile to Rome than others in Britain. Whether this was a voluntary choice or whether the Coritani were cowed into submission by the fate dealt out to other tribes by the Roman legions is not known. What is known is that the arrival of the Romans opened up Leicestershire to organised and steady trade with the Mediterranean world. New foods and ways of preparing them flooded in.

A domestic hog from about 1600. The wild boar was domesticated very early on in the history of agriculture and by the time the animal reached Leicestershire it had lost many of its wild traits.

All varieties of modern chicken are descended from the wild jungle or game fowl, which was first domesticated in India.

One of the key features of the Roman lifestyle that had never before been seen in Britain was the city. In Leicestershire, the first city to be founded was Ratae Corieltauvorum, a name which means 'the walled place of the Coritani'. This was a city built along Roman lines with a forum for business, a basilica for justice and tax collecting and a baths for relaxation. By and large the people who lived in the city were not Romans, but Coritani. The Romans encouraged the wealthier and more noble Celts to live in towns where they could be persuaded to adopt Roman culture – and where the legions could keep an eye on them. The city of Ratae Corieltauvorum would, in time, become Leicester.

The importance of towns for food is that it was in places such as Ratae Corieltauvorum that the first food factories were developed. Watermills introduced were able to grind vast quantities of flour, and bakeries with several ovens were constructed to turn out large quantities of bread. Beer was also brewed on a large scale. The Romans also introduced new types of wheat that could be ground into a finer flour more like that used today. The bread was baked in round loaves about ten inches across that were marked into eight wedge-shaped pieces for ease of cutting into portions – rather like modern pizzas.

The Romans introduced four new types of farm animal, though only two of them has stood the test of time in Leicestershire. Rabbits had been first domesticated in Spain around 200 BC and brought to Britain around AD 100. They were bred in small, walled gardens where they were fed on a carefully controlled diet of grass and vegetables. Rabbits were generally eaten young, with only a few animals destined for breeding allowed to grow to adulthood. Rabbits, of course, soon escaped into the wild and spread across Britain to become a game animal beloved by generations of poachers. The other successful farm animal was the domestic goose, though the place and time where this useful bird was first domesticated is unknown.

The dormouse and the snail never really caught on in Britain – though both were kept in some numbers to appeal to the palates of visitors from the Mediterranean areas of the Roman Empire.

It was during Roman times that a cattle approximating to the modern domestic cow came to Britain. Opinion is divided as to the role played in the production of this beast by native types, but it seems almost certain that the bulk of European breeds are descended from cattle first bred in Roman times in the north-western parts of their Empire – countries that are now Britain, Belgium and France. It is not certain if the Romans brought the peacock to Britain. If they did, it did not prove to be popular.

The evidence for new fruits and vegetables is less easy to come by as, unlike animals, they left behind no bones to be found by archaeologists. Written sources refer to a wide range of plant foods that we would today find familiar, but whether the Romans brought them to Leicestershire or if they found them already here we do not know. Apples, pears, peaches, plums, almonds, chestnuts, onions, radishes, lettuces, marrows, asparagus, cabbages, turnips, leeks, beets and dill are all mentioned by writers at this date.

The main innovation as regards to drink brought in by the Romans was wine. Wine produced in what is now France, Spain and Italy had been imported to Britain in large clay pots called amphorae from around 80 BC onwards and there is some evidence that vines were being grown in southern Britain by the time of Christ. It was not until the Romans arrived, however, that viticulture began in Britain on anything like a large scale. A key element in the success of the grape in what became Leicestershire at this date was the climate, which was then slightly warmer and drier than it is today.

British wines were not highly rated by the Romans and were produced mostly for local consumption. Contemporary writers say that British wine was thin and dry. This might sound like a refreshing summer quaff to the modern eye, but Romans preferred their wines heavy and sweet. One form of British wine that did achieve success was a sweet white wine that was mixed with honey and rose petals before being sealed into amphorae for export.

The Romans introduced two key pieces of cooking equipment not before seen. The first was the iron grill on which food could be grilled. This replaced the spit as a means of cooking smaller joints and cuts of meat over a fire. The other was the spoon, which rapidly became as essential for stirring pots of boiling food as it was for eating liquid foods at table.

In AD 410 the Roman Emperor Honorios found himself beset by an overwhelming range of problems and unable any longer to defend the key heartlands of his empire. He sent a message to the local authorities in Britain telling them that they had to take responsibility for running their own affairs and defending their own lands for the next few years until the Roman Empire was once again strong enough to run things properly. As we now know, the empire was in terminal decline and never came back. At the time, however, everyone thought the situation to be purely temporary and carried on much as before.

The following two centuries saw the survival of Roman administration in Britain for three or more generations, followed by a catastrophic collapse around the year AD 530 which was followed by the formation of English kingdoms across most of Britain and Celtic states to the west and north. Leicester, of course, was one of those areas conquered by the English, though substantial numbers of Romano-Britons survived in this area.

The foods and drinks consumed by the locals were affected not only by the new Germanic rulers but also by a slow, but no less catastrophic, change in climate. The weather across Leicestershire, and everywhere else, became significantly cooler and wetter between around AD 350 and AD 600. Several plant crops that had flourished in Roman times died out. Grapes were the first to go, but others such as cucumbers and figs soon followed.

A royal feast of the thirteenth century. Dishes such as the boar's head shown here were presentational dishes that formed the centrepiece of formal banquets and dinners. They were usually removed from the table to be carved and the meat served to the poorer folk after the event was over.

The climate would become warmer and drier again after about the year 1000, allowing vines to again be grown in Britain as far north as Yorkshire. Other delicate crops again returned to Britain in this warmer medieval period. But they again were banished from Leicestershire when the climate took a fresh turn for the worse after around 1500. The next warming trend of the twentieth century has not yet got the British climate back to its heights of the Roman and medieval periods, but it is on its way. Several vineyards now exist in Leicestershire and are producing some nice wines – though no doubt the Romans would find them too dry.

Meanwhile the new English culture that took a hold on Leicestershire after the collapse of post-Roman rule was shaping the cuisine of the county toward the style with which we are familiar today.

Freshwater fish continued to be a reliable source of food, though not one that was very widespread. In 1350 the Countess of Leicester employed a full time fisherman. His job was not so much to go out with rod and line as to maintain ponds and keep them stocked with fish such as

Not much carp is eaten these days, but up until about 1750 it was often taken from rivers by the poorer members of society to be grilled and eaten.

trout, carp and perch. One stretch of the Soar was given to the citizens of Leicester by a generous landowner, and residents of the city were allowed to fish there free of charge. Preserved sea fish were brought in by cart and river boat – kippers and salt cod were the most popular.

Sheep gradually increased in popularity as a farm animal until by around 1250, there were as many sheep in England as cattle, pigs and goats put together. In Leicestershire sheep were concentrated in the more broken country west of the Soar. Most sheep were kept for their wool or milk, so they were not slaughtered for food until they were fairly old. The meat from such older animals was known as mutton and usually needed to be boiled or slow cooked to be enjoyable. Roasted lamb was a dish only for the rich.

Pork, bacon and ham on the other hand made for good eating even when the animal had foraged loose in the woods for years. It was a favourite with all classes of people. Rural folk liked the pig as it could be fed on scraps and waste, while townsfolk appreciated the fact that it could be kept in a small yard.

Cattle were treated mostly as beasts of burden by the early English, with any beef coming from older animals and therefore very tough. It was not until the thirteenth century that cattle

An illustration from a medieval manuscript showing shepherds looking after their flock. The broken nature of the country is clear. In Leicestershire sheep and goats were kept mostly in the west of the county.

in Leicestershire began to be raised for their meat and milk. Thereafter the local folk increasingly took to eating both beef and dairy products based on cow's milk. The sheep's milk and cheese that had been popular since the fall of Roman Britain went out of favour. Goats soon went out of favour in Leicestershire, remaining popular only in hilly or mountainous regions.

Chickens, ducks and geese continued to be farmed for their eggs and flesh, with chickens gradually becoming the most popular. Game birds continued to be eaten by anyone who could spare the time to go out to catch them. Exactly when pheasants arrived in England is a matter of dispute. Some think that they came in the last days of the Roman Empire, others that they first arrived around AD 900. Certainly they were flapping around Leicestershire by 1100, but not in very great numbers. The modern practice of rearing huge numbers of chicks that are then released into the wild for a season's hunting did not emerge until modern times.

One development during these centuries was that bread began to fall out of favour compared to pottages. Where the Roman had eaten his grain crops mostly as bread, the Englishman preferred to eat his in stews, thick soups and casseroles. The richer nobles might eat bread, but it did not begin to regain favour among the ordinary English until after about 1400. Biscuits, however, increased in popularity. Both savoury and sweet biscuits became staple products for bakers, while after about 1300 pastry in its various forms began to be made and by 1500 was enormously popular as a base for pies, flans, tarts and the like.

Citrus fruits began to be imported to England around 1250, but they remained a food only for the rich. They could not be grown here and survived the journey from the Mediterranean only if brought on fast ships, which pushed the price up. Other fruits could be grown in Leicestershire once their seeds or plants were brought in from Eastern Europe. These included gooseberries, cherries, damsons, medlars, walnuts, quinces and mulberries.

Beer underwent a dramatic transformation about the year 1400. Up until that date beer kept sweet and drinkable for only a few days, so it had to be made fresh on a frequent basis and could not be transported very far. Then a merchant from Flanders shipped up the Thames to London a type of ale that could be kept for weeks, due to it having been infused with a preservative extracted from hops. The hops gave the ale a bitter tang that proved to be hugely popular with drinkers, while brewers appreciated the keeping quantities of the new drink. By 1440 Londoners

An illustration from a medieval manuscript showing haymaking. The preservation of fodder for livestock to eat over the winter was essential if breeding adults were to be kept alive for the next season.

An illustration from a medieval manuscript showing the reaping of wheat. This was the principal grain crop in Leicestershire for over a thousand years.

were drinking more of the new hopped beer than the older-style drink that was becoming known as ale. Within twenty years the popularity of the new beer had reached Leicester and by 1500, beer was the favourite drink of all England.

Indeed, it was about this time that government began to take a disapproving interest in binge drinking and English drunkenness. Bishops tried hard to ban the Sunday drinking sessions known as 'church ales' when each man would bring a jug of beer to pass around his friends once the church service was over. The crackdown failed. England has remained a comparatively heavy drinking kingdom ever since.

The only really important new type of food to enter Leicestershire after hopped beer was the potato, which came from the Americas in the later sixteenth century. Otherwise the farmers and cooks of Leicestershire were pretty well-equipped to begin the production of the foods and dishes for which the county has since become famous.

## *Three*

# TAME AND GAME

Animals have lived wild in Leicestershire since the glaciers retreated back toward Scotland at the end of the last Ice Age – and they have been hunted by humans here for almost as long. Some of the more exciting wild game beasts – such as woolly mammoths, woolly rhinoceros and aurochs – have long since vanished from the county. Others went only to make a comeback in the twentieth century; wild boar for instance is on its way back to the woodlands.

Other game animals have never gone away and have remained a staple of country larders and recipes for generations. These days not everybody is skilled enough at country crafts for it to be easy for them to slip out into the fields for an evening of catching a rabbit or two. Fortunately, however, rabbits, pheasants and other game are usually available at specialist butchers.

But it is the domestic livestock that have for centuries contributed most meat to the kitchens of Leicestershire. For centuries the local farmers bred beasts for their own use, slaughtering most of them in the autumn when the grass stopped growing in the fields and fodder became scarce. More recently livestock has been more carefully bred to produce individual breeds with valued and distinctive characteristics.

There are two important breeds of domestic livestock to take their names from the county of Leicestershire. Both have been of paramount importance to the improved breeding of livestock that took place from the eighteenth century onward, and both are still kept in the county. Perhaps most surprising is the fact that both were bred by the same man.

Robert Bakewell was a yeoman farmer who spent his entire life on the farm at Dishley Mill, just outside Loughborough, that was left to him by his father. He was an imposing figure of a man, standing 5ft 10ins tall and weighing something over sixteen stone of brawny muscle built up by long days of arduous labour on his farm. He was a famously sober and respectable man. He rose every day before dawn to eat breakfast and get out to work. He returned for lunch at one o'clock, then came back to his home at dusk after which he devoted himself to paperwork and reading until supper at nine o'clock, after which he was always in bed by eleven o'clock. Nobody ever heard him swear, and he never worked on a Sunday.

Robert Bakewell was born in 1725 and inherited the farm in 1760. By that date he had already begun experimenting with such newfangled ideas as fertilising his fields, irrigating pasture land and rotating crops. But it had been in 1744 that he had had the flash of genius that would dominate the rest of his life and revolutionise livestock farming across the world. Bakewell's idea seems simple and almost obvious now, but at the time it was revolutionary and treated with great suspicion.

A Leicester ewe as depicted by a Victorian artist. The breed has proved to be one of the most important in the history of sheep breeding, with many modern breeds having the Leicester in their ancestry.

A Leicester ram as depicted by a Victorian artist. The rams of this breed could command astonishingly high stud fees in the late eighteenth century.

Put simply, Bakewell thought that if he bred a ram with good qualities with a ewe which had good qualities, then the lamb that was born was likely to have the same characteristics as its parents. Bakewell divided his grazing land up into numerous small fields, separated by fences and hedges that sheep could not break through. He rigorously divided up his stock so that rams and ewes could not mix at all. He then further divided the flock so that only those animals showing characteristics that he wanted passed onto the lambs were kept, while the rest were sent to market. He then allowed one ram in with one ewe at a time, keeping a careful note of which animal mated with which. He then studied the offspring to see if his theory was working.

What Bakewell was looking for in his sheep was an animal which was neat and compact in body shape, grew rapidly to adult size, had plenty of fat on the carcass and which produced long wool fibres. By 1755 Bakewell felt he had achieved something worth talking about and began inviting other farmers interested in experimental ways of farming to view his livestock. He also began renting out his 'improved' rams for stud purposes. The first year he did this he got 16s per ram. His efforts were costing more than they were bringing in and two years later Bakewell faced bankruptcy. His fellow experimenter farmers, however, thought that his work was worth investing in and put cash into his farm.

A portrait of a bull from the herd bred by Bakewell at his farm just outside Loughborough. These animals gave a particularly fine beef, and their descendants still produce high quality meat to this day.

A cow from the breed developed by Bakewell. The cows gave good quality milk for their day, but the breed's use as a dairy cow has been superseded by more modern varieties.

Their rewards were quick in coming. By 1774 Bakewell had perfected what he called the 'New Leicester' sheep. The breed remains to this day. It has a small head with a face covered in short white hairs and characterised by a large eye, long ears, a tapering neck, straight back and well-arched ribs. The fleece it gives is heavy and has a relatively long staple, while the meat is well flavoured and fatty. It is just what Bakewell set out to produce. In the first year after announcing the new breed, Bakewell was able to charge £840 stud fees for each ram, and the following year he was charging £1,260. His fortune was made.

As soon as he began to achieve results with his sheep, Bakewell began work on cattle. Using the same methods and principles, Bakewell was able to produce the Dishley Longhorn breed of cattle. The breed is brown and white, and characterised by great horns that sweep downward towards the muzzle in an arc. When he started work, the average weight of a beast sent to slaughter was 370lbs, but by the time he announced his new breed in 1786 the weight had more than doubled to 840lbs. Not only that, but the quality of the meat was greatly improved and so brought a higher price per pound.

Bakewell also tried his hand at improving farm horses. His work here was not so successful, largely because he began work on horses rather later than on sheep and cattle. At the time of his death in 1795 the 'improved black cart horse', as he called it was still very much a work in progress. The breeding of these animals was continued by others and by the 1830s had produced the breed known today as the shire horse.

The Longhorn breed of beef cattle is still kept in Leicestershire. The superb quality beef can be found for sale at markets – as shown here – or direct from the Blackbrook Farm.

Bakewell's methods were taken up by other farmers as soon as he had proved its effectiveness. Numerous other breeds of animal have since been produced by Bakewell's methods of selective breeding. These breeding efforts have been massively successful at producing breeds suited to different environments and producing different types of meat, wool and other products. So far have the breeds improved that Bakewell's originals have fallen out of favour; his Leicester sheep was by 2008 down to only around 500 animals worldwide, many of them in Leicester. The Dishley Longhorn cattle has fared rather better. This is largely because its meat remains among the best of any cattle in the world and although it is expensive to rear, it remains profitable.

While sheep and cattle were being bred in the west of Leicestershire, pigs dominated in the east. As early as 1756, Leicestershire was named as one of the three English counties with the most pigs. The county did not produce its own variety of improved pig breed, but relied instead on the Tamworth pig or the English White.

As we shall see in a later chapter, the dairy industry boomed in eastern Leicestershire from the 1700s onward. It was this that made possible the huge number of pigs. The whey left over from cheese production is highly nutritious and when mixed with the malt left over from brewing

Bison are one of the more unusual game animals to be kept in Leicestershire, these animals being found on the Bouverie Lodge farm.

beer, it makes for an almost ideal pig food. Many of these pigs were raised on farms, but others were household pigs that were familiar beasts in both town and country.

Again it was the cheap availability of whey and old malt that made domestic pig keeping so attractive in eastern Leicestershire, but household food scraps were added as well. In rural areas, waste plants from vegetable patches and fruit groves were all thrown into the pig food. Careful owners boiled the food up into swill in order to kill off any bacteria or infections that might harm the pig, but other pig keepers were not so fussy. After all, it was the ability of the pig to eat almost anything and convert it into eatable meat that made it such a useful beast to have around.

In towns the pigs were routinely turned out onto the streets to consume whatever rubbish was left lying about in the gutters. In the days before modern refuse collections or sewers there was usually plenty of rubbish and filth lying about in towns, and the household pigs did a valuable job in clearing a lot of it up. By the later nineteenth century it was counted something of a social disaster to live in a street where the pigs were turned out, but before that it was an accepted part of life in towns such as Market Harborough, Lutterworth, and Oakham in Rutland.

These household pigs were generally bought as piglets from a piggery, then kept for around eight months until they had reached adult size and were ready for slaughter. The most usual form of domestic pig sty was a small yard surrounded by a stout brick or stone wall about five feet high. Inside this was the feeding trough and a roofed over room just large enough for the pig to lie down and turn around in. Owners who cared well for their pigs made sure that the room

**Above left:** A butcher at work on a joint of beef in the Taylor's butcher's shop in Bottesford. The traditional skills of high quality butchering are kept alive in such family businesses as this.

**Above right:** The cool storeroom in the yard behind Taylor's butcher's shop in Bottesford. It is essential that good quality meat – here it is lamb – should be properly hung for several days to ensure that the meat is tender and full of flavour.

**Right:** A breast of lamb (left) and three legs of lamb hang up in the window of Taylor's butchers shop in Bottesford. These days the easy-to-carve prime joints such as leg are most popular, but the breast is equally packed with flavour and if properly cooked is every bit as succulent.

Sheep grazing peacefully on a farm in the eastern part of the county. The collapse in grain prices that occurred during the 1870s as vast quantities of cheap American wheat were imported led many Leicestershire farmers to abandon cereal farming and to take up livestock rearing. Prior to that date, most sheep in Leicestershire had been kept in the west of the county where the land was less suited to grain crops.

was lined with straw, which was changed frequently, and that the pigs droppings were scooped up from the yard and taken off to be used as manure. Pigs are habitually clean animals, only acquiring their reputation for smelly dirtiness when not cared for properly.

Comfortable as a household pig sty might be, no pig was ever content. In the wild, pigs do not feed from troughs. Instead they snuffle about in woodland munching happily on leaves, fruits and shoots from trees or bushes. They root about, turning over the soil with their snouts to search out worms, beetles and buried goodies. If they manage to catch a bird or squirrel, then all to the good. Even the most domesticated of pigs has an irresistible urge to poke about in corners, turn over soil and generally mess about with anything within reach in case it hides something edible. Domestic pigs kept in small sties would inevitably dig holes, undermine walls and sometimes escape to cause havoc in surrounding gardens.

The impulse to root had to be controlled, and it was for this reason that nearly every domestic pig had a ring in its nose. While all pig owners cared for the welfare of their animals in order to get good quality meat at the end of the process, the process of inserting the ring was unavoidably painful. The local blacksmith usually performed the feat in return for a few pennies. He would visit the pig sty with his tools. A rope would be tied around the pig's snout and this would be pulled tight to force the pig's head upward and keep it still. The ring was then opened and inserted into the pig's nostrils. When the pliers forced the ring shut, the sharpened ends cut through the flesh between the nostrils.

The pain to the pig did not end with the insertion of the ring. Every time it lowered its head to root about or pushed against a solid object, the ring was jammed back against the tender nose inflicting pain that caused the pig to stop whatever it was doing. As a method of keeping the householder's property intact, the pig nose ring was perfect. As a humane device, it left a lot to be desired.

The pig keepers of Leicestershire developed a few local habits which marked them out from the rest of the country. The first of these was to refer to the runt of a litter as being the 'Anthony' or the 'Tony'. It is thought that this term derives from the days when people were obliged to pay a tithe, or tenth, of their produce to the Church. St Anthony was the patron saint of livestock, so the animals given to the church became known as St Anthony's beasts. The wily pig breeders of Leicestershire gave the runt to the Church, keeping the rest for themselves.

Another habit in Leicestershire was to throw a shovel of ash from the household fire into the pig sty each morning. More often than not the pig would pounce eagerly on the mixture of ash and cinders and gobble it up. Whether it did the pig any good or not is unclear, but it seemed to be enjoyed. The pigs also seemed to relish the final act on family washing day. After all the clothes had been washed, the woman of the house was in the habit of throwing the dirty, soapy water over the pig. Most pigs, once they got used to the ritual, would come eagerly to the door of the pig sty when they heard the familiar sounds of washing day so as to be ready for their drenching.

When the pig was large enough for slaughter, the local butcher would be called in. As soon as the butcher arrived, and sometimes before he did, the pig began to squeal. The average pig has a very good sense of smell – essential for finding worms and underground roots – so it was easily able to scent the blood on the butcher and his clothes. The pig knew what was coming and was predictably unhappy about it.

The butcher would lead the pig out of the sty to stand on a previously cleaned stretch of yard. Beside the pig was placed a wooden trestle. The pig was then killed and pushed to topple on to the trestle. Before about 1880 most pigs were killed with a poleaxe, a long-handled device that had an axe blade on one side and a stout, sharp spike on the other. Swinging the poleaxe with sufficient force and accuracy to drive the spike through the pig's skull and into its brain to cause instant death was a highly skilled job.

The trestle was then lifted up so that the carcass hung head down to allow the blood to flow out of the slit throat –being carefully collected for the making of black pudding. Meanwhile, the pig was shaved to remove the hairs and bristles. These were again kept and sold to the makers of shaving brushes and other items that needed stiff pig hairs.

The carcass was then slit open for the removal of the internal organs. Most of these were put to one side as offal for use in assorted recipes. This was the moment for which the children of the family and neighbouring houses had been waiting. The bladder was extracted and blown up by the butcher to form a balloon-like football that instantly became the centre of a host of traditional games. The carcass was then left to drain overnight before it was ready to be butchered and cut up.

One of the problems with the keeping of household pigs was that the family suddenly had a glut of meat. A good sized pig can produce a huge amount of meat which, if it is not used up, will quickly go off. One solution was for the householders of a village to agree in advance who would slaughter their pig on which day. This would allow the families to pass around the meat and offal to each other, ensuring that everybody had a share of everybody else's pig.

Another solution was to find ways of storing the pork so that it did not go off. It was in this activity that the householders of Leicestershire excelled and ultimately became famous.

The legs and flitches, or sides, of the carcass were often converted into bacon and ham. First the cuts were trimmed of excess fat or loose pieces of meat. Then they were laid out in a trough, sometimes the very one from which the pig had been fed. The meat was vigorously rubbed with a mixture of fifty parts salt to one part saltpetre until the grains had been pushed into every nook and cranny of the meat. The joints were then covered over with the mixture and left. Sides were usually left for two weeks, after which they were taken out, rubbed down and then covered again with a fresh batch of salt for a third week. Legs were kept under salt for four or six weeks, depending on how big they were.

The joints were then hung up for a further three or four weeks. In rural areas where wood was plentiful, the joints were usually hung in smoke houses, but in urban areas they were habitually hung over the coal-fired stove where they would be warm and dry but out of reach of the coal smoke. The two processes produced respectively smoked and unsmoked bacon and ham.

The less popular cuts of pork could be stored for up to two years by being salted down in barrels. The technique was fairly straightforward. The pork was cut into strips about an inch wide and rubbed all over with the same salt and saltpetre mixture as used for curing hams. A barrel was then brought in and a layer of salt mix about an inch deep put across the bottom. Pieces of pork were then put in to form a layer, which was then covered over with salt mix. Another layer of pork followed, then another of salt mix and so on until the barrel was full. A wooden disc was put on top of the top layer of salt and on top of that a heavy weight. Every day for the next month or so the weight and wooden disc had to be lifted and more salt mixture poured in. Over time the salt sucked the moisture out of the meat until the salt mixture was reduced to a thick, gooey brine. When the salt had stopped subsiding, a fresh layer of salt was pushed hard down into the top of the barrel and an airtight lid fixed on. This process produced the salt pork which was a staple food of sailors from Roman times down to the invention of tinned food in the mid-nineteenth century.

The off-cuts of pork that were not salted down could be processed in a number of ways. One of the most popular of these has been the sausage. Traditionally there were two types of sausage produced in Leicestershire. The first saw minced meat mixed with an equal quantity of minced fat. This mixture was then mixed with pepper, chopped fat and herbs before being stuffed firmly into the cleaned intestines of the pig. It was crucial to ensure that the stuffing was as dense as possible to exclude air. The resulting sausage was then smoked. The process was designed to exclude air from the meat and if done properly, the resulting salami-type sausage would keep for some weeks.

The second type of sausage is the one with which most people in Britain are familiar today. This variety saw mixed meat and fat minced up before being mixed with breadcrumbs or rolled grains and a blend of herbs and spices. The resulting sausage meat was then stuffed into the intestines. These sausages were cooked within a day or two and were really a convenient method of using up odd scraps of meat and making them go further.

These sausages had been made as early as Roman times, but it was not until the 1630s that a butcher in London began giving the length a periodic twist to form the links of sausages with which we are so familiar today. The practice spread rapidly and was found in Leicester by the 1660s.

Another favourite product of the household pig was the pork pie. We shall look at the development of the household pork pie into the Melton Mowbray pork pie – the famed 'King of Pies' – in the next chapter, but the key point about pork pies in their early days was that they helped to preserve meat for a few days or weeks. The act of cooking chopped meat in a pie preserved it and killed off any bacteria and encased the meat in a pastry that was more resistant to spoiling infections from the air than the cooked meat within. When a pie was intended to be kept for some time, melted lard was poured into it after cooking to fill up any gaps between the meat and the crust. This excluded air from the meat and allowed it to keep in a cool larder for a surprisingly long time.

Thus equipped with a range of meats, cooking techniques and preserving methods, the cooks of Leicestershire went to work to create a variety of dishes to use the meats they produced.

# Pork and Apple Pie

| Serves 4 | Preparation time: 20 minutes | Cooking time: 1 hour 30 minutes |
|---|---|---|

This dish from the 1780s seems to be designed as a way of using up leftover roast pork. It was then usual to roast a large joint on a Sunday and to carve slices from the joint cold in the days that followed. Of course, anyone could get bored with yet another slice of cold meat, so various ways of livening up the leftovers were developed, and this was one.

## Ingredients

1lb cold cooked pork
1lb cooking apples
½ pt cider or ale
½lb shortcrust pastry

## Method

❖ Cut the pork into cubes about half an inch across.

❖ Peel and core the apples, then slice them thinly.

❖ Take a pie dish and place a layer of pork pieces across the bottom. On top of this place a layer of apple slices. Then add another layer of pork, followed by another of apple and so on until all the pork and apple is used up.

❖ Add the cider or ale to the dish.

❖ Roll out the pastry to a sheet big enough to cover the pie dish.

❖ Cover the pie dish with the pastry, cutting a hole in the centre to allow steam to escape.

❖ Bake in a moderate oven (180°C/Gas Mark 4) for an hour or an hour and a half.

❖ Serve hot.

# Melton Market Day Savoury

| Serves 6 | Preparation time: 25 minutes | Cooking time: 4 hours or more |
|---|---|---|

The lady who gave me this recipe told me that it came from a farm and was intended to be left cooking in the simmering oven of a range while everyone was out at the market. It would be ready to eat when the family got home. I suppose the modern equivalent would be a slow cooker, but it works equally well in a cool oven.

## Ingredients

1 ½lb potatoes, peeled and thickly sliced
4 onions, peeled and sliced
1 apple, peeled, cored and sliced
2 pig's kidneys, sliced
8oz tomatoes, skinned and chopped
6 pork chops
1 teaspoon dried sage
½ pt stock or water

## Method

❖ In a large casserole dish lay down a layer of potatoes.

❖ Then layer in the pork chops, kidneys, apple and onion.

❖ Top with another layer of potatoes.

❖ Add the stock or water.

❖ Cook in a low oven (150°C/Gas Mark 2) for 4 hours or longer if preferred.

# Game Soup

Serves 4　　　　Preparation time: About 30 minutes　　　　Cooking time: 4 hours

This rich and hearty soup can be made with any sort of smaller game, but rabbit or pheasant are best. The soup is cooked in two fairly lengthy stages, so I prefer to prepare it one day and serve it up the next.

## Ingredients

2lb game joints
1 onion
1 carrot
1 turnip
6 sticks of celery
1 teaspoon ground ginger
1 teaspoon pepper
1 teaspoon salt
Rosemary & Thyme
4 pts stock
1 wineglass of sherry
Butter

## Method

❖ Remove as much meat as possible from bones and set aside.
❖ Chop the onion, carrot, turnip and celery.
❖ Put the chopped vegetables and bones into a saucepan with the stock, salt, pepper, rosemary and thyme.
❖ Bring to the boil, then cover tightly and simmer for three hours.
❖ Strain the liquid, discarding the bones and vegetables.
❖ Cut the meat into small pieces and fry in the butter until well browned.
❖ Add the meat to the stock, bring to the boil and simmer for one hour.
❖ Add the sherry and return briefly to the boil.
❖ Serve hot with buttered toast.

# Pheasant in Port

Serves 2　　　　Preparation time: 10 minutes　　　　Cooking time: 1 hour

There are several extensive and well stocked pheasant shoots in Leicestershire. But you don't need to go out with a gun, as these days you can find pheasant in a range of butchers shops and even supermarkets. The season runs from October to February. Most modern birds are fairly young and can be roasted, but if you are worried your bird might be a bit tough you should stew it instead. If you feel that using port is unduly lavish, substitute red wine instead.

## Ingredients

1 pheasant, jointed
1oz butter
¼ bottle of port
Salt and pepper
1 tablespoon redcurrant jelly

## Method

❖ In a deep pan gently fry the pheasant pieces in the butter until they are nicely golden.
❖ Add the port and seasoning.
❖ Bring gently to the boil.
❖ Cover tightly and simmer for an hour, or until tender.
❖ Stir in the redcurrant jelly.
❖ Serve hot with jacket potatoes or rice.

# Grilled Pheasant Bites

**Serves 4**   **Preparation time: 15 minutes**   **Cooking time: 20 minutes**

Although this recipe sounds remarkably like a variation on the sort of modern chicken nuggets or dippers that are served in host of fast food restaurants, it actually comes from a nineteenth-century collection of game recipes. I would imagine that only a young, tender bird would be suitable for this dish. In the original it is described as being 'served hot to table at breakfast', but that must have been for somebody who was going to be working outside all day. For modern palates I would have thought this to be a supper dish.

## Ingredients
1 pheasant
Lard
1 egg
3oz breadcrumbs
Salt
Cayenne or powdered chilli

## Method
❖ Joint the pheasant into small, neat pieces.
❖ Gently fry the pieces in the lard until half cooked.
❖ Meanwhile, mix the salt and cayenne or chilli in with the breadcrumbs and beat the egg in a bowl.
❖ Remove the pheasant pieces from the pan and drain.
❖ Dip each pheasant piece in the beaten egg, then dredge with the breadcrumb mixture.
❖ Grill the pieces under a moderate heat for 10 minutes.

# Venison Stew

**Serves 4**   **Preparation time: 20 minutes**   **Cooking time: 2 hours**

Wild venison was often fairly tough so only the choicest cuts were roasted, and those were usually served to richer folk. The less well off had the tougher joints that needed long, slow cooking and – as here – marinating to make them tender. There are not many wild deer in Leicestershire these days, but there is at least one farm that raises them free range – and some butchers stock cuts brought in from elsewhere.

## Ingredients
2lb venison
1 pt beer
1lb parsnips or turnips, thickly sliced
2oz butter
1oz flour
Salt & pepper
2oz sugar

## Method
❖ Cut the venison into pieces about ½ inch across.
❖ Place venison and beer into a bowl, cover and leave for at least 3 hours.
❖ Remove the meat from the beer.
❖ Gently fry the parsnips or turnip in the butter, then place in a casserole dish
❖ Toss the meat in the flour, then fry in the butter until browned, then place on top of the vegetables.
❖ Add the beer marinade and sugar to the frying pan to collect the cooking juices. Bring gently to the boil, then add to the casserole.
❖ Place casserole in a moderate oven (180°C/Gas Mark 4) for two hours.
❖ Serve hot with boiled potatoes.

# Roast Meat Pudding

**Serves 4**      **Preparation time: 10 minutes**      **Cooking time: 30 or 40 minutes**

Everybody loves a roast lunch, but in Leicestershire there was a traditional twist to the meal that for some unaccountable reason has fallen out of fashion. Instead of serving potatoes with the meat and other vegetables, the cook would serve up this baked pudding which soaks up the gravy like nothing else. If you can't do without your roast potatoes, halve the quantities for the pudding and have your roasties as well.

## Ingredients

12oz self-raising flour
10oz chopped suet
Salt
Milk

## Method

❖ Mix the flour and suet in a large bowl with a pinch of salt.
❖ Add milk gradually while mixing to produce a soft dough.
❖ Turn the dough on to a floured surface and shape into a circle or oval.
❖ Place dough on to a greased baking tray.
❖ Bake in the oven along with the meat for 30 or 40 minutes, or until risen and golden brown.

# Beef Toads

**Serves 6**      **Preparation time: 25 minutes**      **Cooking time: 50 minutes**

This is a variation on the English classic, Toad in the Hole.

## Ingredients

1lb minced beef
6oz breadcrumbs
2 onions, peeled and finely chopped
1 teaspoon dried mixed herbs
1 egg, beaten
6oz plain flour
1 egg
¾ pt of milk

## Method

❖ In a bowl mix together the minced beef, finely chopped onion, dried herbs, salt, pepper and breadcrumbs. If necessary, bind with a beaten egg.
❖ Separate the meat mixture into 12 pieces and mould into round balls by rolling in the hands.
❖ In a fresh bowl place the flour and add the egg, mixing gently.
❖ Gradually add the milk a little at a time, while mixing into the flour and egg to create a smooth batter.
❖ Place the meatballs into a greased roasting tin.
❖ Pour the batter over the meatballs.
❖ Bake in a hot oven (200°C/Gas Mark 6) for 50 minutes or until the batter has risen and browned nicely.

# Hunting Beef

Fox hunting has been a hugely popular sport in Leicestershire for generations and has shaped the cuisine of the county in many ways. One of the problems with hunting, from the cook's point of view, is that you can never be entirely certain when you will be back. This dish is a good one for hunters as the cooking time is fairly elastic. If the riders are an hour or so late, it will not matter too much.

## Ingredients

Brisket of beef, boned and rolled, allow 6oz per person
Carrots, thickly sliced, allow 8oz per person
Beer, approx 3pts
Sage
Salt and pepper

## Method

❖ Place the brisket into a large saucepan together with all other ingredients.

❖ Bring gently to the boil and then allow to simmer for a minimum of two hours and no more than four hours.

❖ Remove the meat from the saucepan.

❖ Serve the broth as a starter.

❖ Carve the beef and serve with thick slices of bread and butter.


# Quorn Bacon Pudding

This is another classic Leicestershire dish to be born out of the hunting field. Again, cooking time is fairly elastic allowing for the hungry men to turn up late and not have their meal ruined. The dish is traditionally associated with the Quorn Hunt and is usually said to have been devised to the benefit of the hunt staff, not the huntsmen themselves. They don't know what they have been missing! I have seen various versions of this dish, but this is the one I like best.

## Ingredients

10oz self-raising flour
5oz chopped suet
Salt
Water
1lb bacon
2 onions
Sage
1 tablespoon Golden Syrup

## Method

❖ In a mixing bowl, stir together the flour and suet with a pinch of salt.

❖ Slowly add water to make a soft dough.

❖ Divide the dough in two pieces, one piece twice as large as the other.

❖ Gently roll out the larger piece of dough and use it to line a well-greased 3 pint pudding basin.

❖ Roughly chop the onions and bacon.

❖ Place the onion and bacon into the lined pudding basin in alternate layers.

❖ Pour the Golden Syrup over the bacon and onion.

❖ Roll out the smaller piece of dough to form a lid to the pudding, moistening the edges to make it seal securely.

- ❖ Cover the pudding basin with foil, secured with string.
- ❖ Place the pudding basin in a large saucepan of water that reaches about half way up the basin.
- ❖ Bring gently to the boil and then simmer for three hours or so.
- ❖ Remove the basin from the saucepan.
- ❖ Turn the pudding out on to a large plate.
- ❖ Serve piping hot.

## Mutton Pies

| Serves 4 | Preparation time: 40 minutes | Cooking time: 25 minutes |
|---|---|---|

This recipe comes from a gentleman's magazine of the later eighteenth century as a way to use up cold, leftover mutton. I find it works just as well with lamb. This is a cracking way to use up leftovers on a Monday after roasting a joint on Sunday. I have not tried it with beef, pork or chicken but suspect it would work as well with those meats as with lamb.

### Ingredients
1lb shortcrust pastry
8oz cold, cooked mutton or lamb, chopped
Cold gravy
1 small onion, chopped
Milk

### Method
- ❖ Roll out the pastry fairly thinly.
- ❖ Grease a baking tray intended for small jam tarts
- ❖ Cut out the pastry into rounds of the appropriate sizes to form bases and lids for the jam tart tray.
- ❖ Line each tart base with a round of pastry.
- ❖ Add some chopped meat and onion plus a teaspoon of cold gravy.
- ❖ Add the lid to each small pie, using milk to ensure a good seal.
- ❖ Brush the top of each pie with milk.
- ❖ Bake in a hot oven (200°C/Gas Mark 6) for 25 minutes or until golden brown.

## Stuffed Breast of Mutton

| Serves 4 | Preparation time: 20 minutes | Cooking time: 1 hour |
|---|---|---|

This is another dish designed for mutton that works just as well – if not better – with lamb. Breast of lamb is an odd shape that baffles some cooks, but it is ideal when prepared in this way. The cheaper cuts of meat have gone out of fashion over the past decade or so, but they are among the most nutritious and flavoursome that you can find.

### Ingredients
1 breast of lamb
4oz breadcrumbs
Rosemary
2oz chopped dried apricots
Salt and pepper

### Method
- ❖ In a bowl mix together the breadcrumbs, apricots and seasoning. If necessary, bind with some beaten egg.
- ❖ Lay the breast of lamb out flat.
- ❖ Spread the stuffing mix over the meat.

- ❖ Roll up the lamb like a swiss roll and tie securely with string. Do not roll the meat too tightly or the stuffing will ooze out during cooking.
- ❖ Roast in a moderate oven (180°C/Gas Mark 4) for 1 hour.

# Stuffed Pork Belly

| Serves 6 | Preparation time: 20 minutes | Cooking Time: 2 hours |
|---|---|---|

This cheap cut of pork fell out of favour for a while, but has made a comeback in the form of 'Chinese spare ribs'. Supermarkets won't stock these old fashioned joints, but a good family butcher will do so – and he will be happy to trim and prepare it for you.

## Ingredients

3lb pork belly, boned and with rind scored.
4oz breadcrumbs
1 cooking apple, peeled, cored and grated
Salt
Pepper

## Method

- ❖ In a bowl mix together the breadcrumbs, grated apple and seasoning. If necessary, bind with some beaten egg.
- ❖ Lay the port out flat, rind side down.
- ❖ Spread the pork with the stuffing mix.
- ❖ Roll up the pork and tie securely with string. Do not roll the meat too tightly or the stuffing will ooze out during cooking.
- ❖ Rub salt into the exposed pork rind to make for good crackling.
- ❖ Roast in a moderate oven (180°C/Gas Mark 4) for 2 hours.

# Trout with Mushrooms

| Serves 4 | Preparation time: 30 minutes | Cooking time: 30 minutes |
|---|---|---|

The trout is one of the freshwater fish that you will be able to find easily enough in supermarkets.

## Ingredients

4 trout, cleaned
8oz mushrooms, chopped
1 onion, chopped
1 oz butter
Parsley chopped
Salt and pepper
1 lemon

## Method

- ❖ Fry the onion in the butter until soft, but not browned.
- ❖ Add the mushrooms to the pan and fry until soft.
- ❖ Stir in most of the chopped parsley and remove from the heat.
- ❖ Stuff the fish with the onion/mushroom mixture.
- ❖ Place each fish on to a piece of greased aluminium foil. Close the foil up loosely and place all four fish into one roasting tin.
- ❖ Bake in a moderate oven (180°C/Gas Mark 4) for 30 minutes.
- ❖ Meanwhile, slice the lemons.
- ❖ When cooked, remove the trout from the foil and put on plates with the lemon and remaining parsley as a garnish.

# Baked Eels

Eels have not been popular in the twentieth century, but in the Middle Ages they were the food of kings (King John famously died after eating too many of them in one go) and they remained popular into Queen Victoria's reign. In the twenty-first century they have staged a modest comeback among the more daring chefs and sophisticated restaurants, so perhaps it is time to revive this Leicestershire dish dating from the 1880s.

## Ingredients

1lb eels
Parsley, chopped
1 onion, peeled and chopped
1 teaspoon ground nutmeg
2oz sausage meat
Juice of 1 lemon
½lb shortcrust pastry
1oz plain flour
1oz butter
½ pt milk
Salt and pepper

## Method

❖ Skin and wash the eels, then cut them into pieces 2 inches long.

❖ Line the base of a pie dish with the sausage meat

❖ Place the eels on top of the sausage meat together with the onion, nutmeg and lemon juice.

❖ Roll out the pastry to fit as a cover over the pie dish and use to cover the eels.

❖ Place in a moderate oven (180°C/Gas Mark 4) for an hour.

❖ Meanwhile, melt the butter in a pan and add the flour, stirring briskly.

❖ Allow the mixture to bubble for 2 or 3 minutes, but not to change colour.

❖ Remove from the heat and gently stir in half the milk.

❖ Return to the heat until the mixture begins to thicken.

❖ Add the rest of the milk and continue to stir to form a thick white sauce.

❖ Remove the eel pie from the oven, cut into portions and serve with the white sauce.

*Four*

# MELTON MOWBRAY – THE 'KING OF PIES'

Pork pies have been made in England for centuries. Something like a pork pie – it was more like a pork pasty to be honest – was being baked by English cooks from around AD 750, perhaps a little earlier. Round pies baked in metal pie tins and filled with pork were being produced by 1450 when one book mentions them as being eaten at a dinner. These pies would have been baked to preserve the meat they contained. The pastry case was sometimes considered to be superfluous and richer diners were in the habit of casting it aside.

By Tudor times small meat pies were commonly sold in markets as tasty snacks for workmen and labourers. By the 1750s, pie sellers often had small charcoal-fired braziers so that they could heat up the pies to be eaten as soon as they were sold.

Two of Brockleby's Melton Mowbray pork pies ready for serving. The thick, robust crust and the jelly that fills the space around the meat were both essential to the early success of the 'King of Pies'.

Tasty and nutritious as all these pies no doubt were, they lacked a certain something. Nobody thought of them as anything special, nobody wrote home about them and nobody gave them a title. All that was to change in the Leicestershire town of Melton Mowbray sometime around 1780, when an unknown genius had a brilliant idea and so created the Melton Mowbray pork pie: undisputedly the 'King of Pies'.

But to understand why it was in Melton Mowbray that the particular circumstances came together to make the conditions right for the magnificent invention, it is necessary to take a step back and look at two very different industries as they were in Leicestershire the 1740s.

The first was the dairy industry, and in particular cheesemaking. This was booming at the time for various reasons, and was producing a glut of the by-product, whey, which was an ideal pig food. This in turn led to a boom in the production of pork in eastern Leicestershire. A lot of this meat was made into pork pies and sold at the markets in the county's towns. As yet, however, there was nothing to mark these pies out as anything special other than the quantities in which they were made.

The other industry undergoing change was the arable farming that covered most of the clay-based soils of eastern Leicestershire and the low land of the Soar Valley. Until the early eighteenth century, the land in these areas had been farmed along fairly traditional lines. Grain crops predominated, with fruit and vegetable crops grown to supply the towns taking a secondary role. Most villages were surrounded by vast open fields, extensive hay meadows, unfenced woods and rough grazing. Some of this land was shared out among the villagers each year according to traditional formulae. Other stretches of land were owned in common by the villagers. Still other tracts were owned by the lords of the manor, but the villagers had traditional rights of access and use that they exercised in return for a fee, usually quite small.

In the early 1500s, however, a process began which has become known as enclosure. Although the process varied over time and from place to place, the general trend remained the same. Instead of the land being used and apportioned along traditional lines, often being parcelled out between the various farmers each year, the land was instead parcelled up and divided among the farmers on a permanent basis. Each farmer was allotted a set section of land that became his to own and to have the exclusive use of. The new landowners usually enclosed their land with fences or hedgerows to show its boundaries, and so the process became known as enclosure.

The big winners of the enclosure process were the lords of the manor. The great tracts of rough pasture, woodland and meadow that they owned had previously not brought in much money. The traditional rights of the villagers to graze animals or gather hay were paid for by traditionally fixed sums of money or services. But under the new system, the landlord owned the land outright. He could charge what he liked for the right to graze animals. Or he could farm the land himself and forbid the local villagers from using it at all.

Each village family was allotted some of the farmland and were sometimes given cash payments to recompense them for the loss of grazing rights. The more prosperous farmers, or those who saw the merits of the new system quicker than others, were able to take advantage of the new system of land ownership to improve their land by draining it or fertilising it. New fields could be bought and farms expanded. Other villagers, however, lost out. Either way, enclosure stripped them of their benefits or they did not realise how to profit from the new system and sank into poverty.

The enclosures therefore proved to be hugely controversial. Some rural folk welcomed them, others hated them. Riots broke out in Leicestershire in the early 1600s and the unrest over the reforms to land ownership has been blamed in part for the outbreak of the English Civil War. The victory of Parliament in the Civil War meant that the new class of land owners was in the driving seat in place of the king and traditional landowning nobility. The pace of enclosure quickened and by 1720 most of Leicestershire had been enclosed. The rest would follow by 1780.

The new face of farming transformed the landscape. Where there had previously been vast open fields, great tracts of grazing and large stretches of woodland, there were now thousands of small fields separated by hedges and drained by ditches.

In 1753 one of the new class of Leicestershire landowners, Hugo Maynell of Quorndon Hall, had an idea. Meynell was at the time the master of the Leicestershire huntsmen. The new shape of the landscape was causing problems for huntsmen. Deer had previously been an important quarry for the noblemen and gentry. Not only did killing the animal result in a useful carcass that could be divided up and eaten, but the fast-running deer had the stamina to lead the mounted hunters on a good long chase. Foxes were also hunted, but mostly by farmers seeking to eradicate a pest. These fox hunts were often undertaken on foot and the fox was as likely to be shot as it was to be killed by the hounds.

What Meynell realised was that the fox could replace the deer as the quarry of choice for the mounted gentleman hunter. The new Leicestershire countryside with its hedges and ditches would test not only the speed and stamina, but also the jumping abilities of the huntsmen and their horses. The new sport of mounted foxhunting would be faster, more challenging and more exciting than the older sports of mounted deer hunts or foot fox hunts.

Fox hunting in Leicestershire as shown in a Victorian engraving. It was the rapid increase in the popularity of foxhunting that created the demand for the Melton Mowbray pork pie.

Meynell set about training his huntsmen and his hounds to hunt foxes at high speed. He soon realised that whereas the farmers had been mostly interested in killing the foxes, his new style of huntsmen were more interested in the thrill of the chase and the challenge of riding fast over jumps and broken ground. To achieve this, Meynell actually needed to keep a fairly large population of healthy foxes, not exterminate them as had been the previous goal of the farmers. Meynell set about winning over the farmers to the idea of having foxes on their land. He persuaded them that the influx of large numbers of sportsmen to the area would be good for business – what we would today call tourism – and offered them financial inducements.

Soon the Leicestershire landscape was changing again. Small copses of woodland were planted to provide coverts where foxes could live. Hedgerows were widened and given rough grass borders to allow foxes to slink along and hunt successfully. Hedges were managed so that they were dense enough to be impenetrable to a sheep or cow, but low enough to be jumped by a man on a horse. Road and lanes were widened to allow a rider to come over one hedge and have time to position his horse to jump out again the other side. Meynell also took to breeding hounds that could follow the scent of fox on the run for long distances, creating the modern foxhound breed as he did so.

When Meynell took over the old style hunt he averaged three or four riders at each meeting. At one meeting he held in 1791, no fewer than 300 riders turned out. The new sport of foxhunting was a huge success. This was, it should be remembered, a time when the horse was the only way to get about if you did not want to walk. Both the railway and the motor car were a long way in the future. Young men, and later young women, who wanted to show off their skills at riding and the quality of their horses flocked to the foxhunting field. It is difficult to look dashing and brave trotting down Leicester High Street, but much easier when galloping across a field and clearing a hedge in a flying leap.

Soon the two other hunts in Leicestershire followed the lead of the Quorn and were hunting foxes in the new style. The Cottesmore Hunt rode over lands to the east of the Quorn, while the Granby Hunt rode lands north of both. The Granby Hunt is now better known as the Belvoir Hunt, as it is based at Belvoir Castle. At this time the Granby Hunt was run by John Manners, the Marquess of Granby, one of the most colourful and popular figures of his day.

Granby was the eldest son and heir of the Duke of Rutland and in 1741 he became an MP for Grantham, a seat which usually elected whichever candidate had the support of the Duke. His heart, however, was with his military career. He served with distinction against the Highland Rising led by Bonnie Prince Charlie and in 1758 was appointed Colonel of the Royal Horse Guards (The Blues).

The following year Granby took his regiment to war and proved to be a bold and successful commander. At the Battle of Minden, Granby was leading his regiment forward to attack the French when he was stopped by his commander, Sackville. The two officers had a blazing row on the battlefield, and a subsequent inquiry saw Sackville dismissed – though Granby had spoken in his favour. Granby took over command of the British cavalry and led his men to stunning victories at Warburg in 1760 and Villinghausen in 1761. His French opponent bought a portrait of him so that he could study Granby's character. There were plenty of portraits to be had, for Granby was a hugely popular man. Not only did his victories gain him support, but his care for the rank and file among the soldiers was legendary. He famously gave men of good character who had to leave the army due to wounds enough money to start up a small business. Many chose to buy a pub, and named it in his honour – which is why there are so many Marquess of Granby pubs in England to this day.

By 1769 Granby had risen to be Commander in Chief of the British Army, but the following year he fell out with the government and resigned his army position. Granby returned to Leicestershire, where he was able to devote himself more properly to foxhunting. One of the more pressing problems facing the hunt authorities at this date was the question of territory. Paying farmers to maintain their land and hedges in a manner that produced a healthy fox population and good riding was expensive. Each hunt was keen to have its own lands to hunt and did not want other hunts making too free a use of the same area.

The masters of the Quorn, Cottesmore and Granby hunts therefore got out a map and carved up Leicestershire between them. The territories of the three hunts met at the little market town of Melton Mowbray.

As a result of this dividing up of hunting country, Melton Mowbray became extremely busy with huntsmen. More hunt meetings were held there than anywhere else. More huntsmen stayed overnight there than anywhere else. The town fairly hummed with huntsmen, hunt staff and hunting related matters. And this was not a scene akin to modern hunting, which is a preserve of country types. Everyone hunted. The horse was the only way to get about, so anyone who wanted to display their horsemanship and their horse would go hunting. The richest urban dwellers went hunting. And they did not simply show off their riding. They attended balls in their best clothes, flashed off their jewellery and bid to out do each other in the celebrity stakes.

Melton Mowbray became something like a cross between Le Mans when the twenty-four hour motor race is on, combined with the Paris catwalk fashion shows, some celebrity party packed with A-listers and a policy meeting of the country's leading politicians. It was all go in Melton Mowbray.

There was soon one simple matter related to hunting that began to cause problems - lunch. Hunts would designate a meeting place, so everybody knew where they would be eating breakfast. And most huntsmen had arranged to stay either at a friend's house or at an inn, so that they were reasonably certain of where they would be eating dinner. But lunch was a problem. Given the vagaries of chasing a fox, nobody setting out for a day's hunting knew where they were going to be at lunchtime. If they were near an inn which happened to have a good stock of food, then all well and good. But all too often inns were either absent, or did not have enough food to satisfy over a hundred hungry huntsmen who suddenly turned up.

Riders took to stashing food in the deep, capacious pockets of their riding jackets. But this in itself was a bit of a problem. Given that the riders spent a lot of time galloping about and jumping over hedges, anything in a coat pocket was going to be bashed about a fair bit. Bread rolls and lumps of hard cheese might survive such a pounding, as could firm apples, but not much else.

Which was when somebody baking a pork pie in Melton Mowbray had their brilliant idea, which was this. If he or she baked a pie that was the right size to go into a riding coat pocket, but was tough enough to stand up to the pounding, then they could sell it to huntsmen to take with them to eat for lunch. To produce such a pie took a degree of skill and some thought.

At the time, most meat pies were shaped more like a modern Cornish pasty. The shape was not suitable for the tough handling that a pie in a pocket was going to get on a foxhunt. The pointed ends broke off almost immediately. What was needed was a shape without corners. The round pie with flat base and lid was soon developed.

The pie was made in a unique way. A pastry known as hot water pastry was developed. This pastry was easy to mould to shape, but when baked was much harder and less likely to flake than any other type of pastry. This pastry was certainly in use by 1790, and seems to have been an established part of the process by then. The ball of hot water pastry was shaped when it was warm by being gently massaged by hand up the sides of an empty bottle. This gave it its unique round, flat-bottomed shape. And given the hard-drinking habits of the Marquess of Granby and many other huntsmen, there were plenty of empty bottles knocking about in Melton Mowbray at the time.

When the bottle was removed from the pastry case, the space left behind was filled with meat. There was really only one meat of choice that could be used. Given the huge number of pigs being kept in the area due to the booming dairy trade, good quality pork was readily available in quantity and at a reasonable price. So into the pie it went.

It was not only the shape that could make a pie vulnerable to being knocked to pieces. If there is a gap between the pie crust and the meat filling, this will allow a blow to buckle the pastry inward and so break it up more easily. Meat inevitably shrinks when it is cooked, so most pies have just this sort of a gap. Pies that were baked to store the meat had previously been filled up after baking with melted lard to fill the gaps and exclude air from touching the meat. But the pies being baked for the huntsmen were to be eaten within a day or two of being baked, so the lard was not needed. In any case, nobody really wants to sink their teeth into a succulent looking pie only to be rewarded with a mouthful of greasy lard.

It came about that in place of the lard a jelly was poured in to the pie. This jelly was made by boiling up the bones, trotters and offcuts of the slaughtered pig in a vat for two hours or more. The offcuts and trotters gave the resulting liquid flavour, while the bones contributed gelatine which would cause the liquid to turn to a solid jelly when it cooled. When this was poured hot into the pie through a hole in the crust as it came out of the oven, it filled all the gaps between meat and crust with a delicious jelly that at the same time made the pie a solid and robust product that would stand up to being bounced around in a pocket for hours on end.

The Melton Mowbray pork pie had been born. Its rise to greatness was yet to come.

For some years the hunting fraternity bought the Melton Mowbray pork pie in increasing quantities from the various bakers of the town. By 1820 the pie was certainly something of an industry in its own right. Production was booming as the pie came to be demanded not only by huntsmen about to set off on a day's hunt, but also by huntsmen wanting something tasty for supper, or for breakfast for that matter.

By the 1820s one problem with the production process began to be evident. There was a small, but consistent, wastage of pastry caused by the bottles breaking as the hot pastry was moulded up against them. The shattered glass got into the pastry, which then had to be thrown away. The solution was produced by a Mrs Dickinson – a name that would remain important to the Melton Mowbray pork pie right through to the present day.

Mrs Dickinson carved a solid wooden 'dolly' in the shape of the bottom half of a wine bottle and added a handle to the top. Mrs Dickinson began moulding the pastry cases for her pies around her wooden dolly. The other bakers saw the advantages of the wooden dolly. Not only were there no breakages, but pies could now be produced in any size required. Soon every Melton Mowbray pork pie was made around a dolly, and this remains the case today.

The next stage in the development of the pie was down to a baker named Edward Alcock, a postmaster named Edward Burbridge and a stagecoach guard whose name was unfortunately not recorded. The prime mover in the business deal that followed was Edward Alcock, who ran a bakery in what is now Leicester Street. Alcock had invested heavily in the equipment necessary for making pork pies and had hired staff with the necessary skills. Because the Melton Mowbray

4. The dolly is removed to leave behind the crust of the pie. It will be essential in later stages that the base and sides are solid and have no gaps through which the molten jelly might leak out.

5. The chopped and seasoned pork is placed into the pie shell. The pastry is then patted gently up against the meat to ensure the tightest possible fit.

6. The pie lid is put on and gently massaged into place so that it is tightly sealed against the crust sides. It is then crimped to ensure that it remains firmly in place during baking.

7. The final crimping of the pastry is completed so that the pie under construction can join the two in the foreground that are ready to go into the oven for baking.

**The stages in the making of a Melton Mowbray pork pie as demonstrated by a master pie maker from Brockelby's Pie Shop.**

1. A piece of the special pastry is kneaded to ensure that it is of the correct temperature and consistency.

2. The wooden dolly is pushed into the ball of pastry to start the process of raising the pie crust.

3. The pie crust is raised up the sides of the wooden dolly with the fingers until it reaches the horizontal line etched on to the dolly to indicate the correct size.

pork pie as it had developed by the 1820s was filled with jelly that lacked the preservative qualities of lard, the products did not keep for more than a few days. That meant that on the rare occasions when several days went by without a hunt meeting in or near Melton Mowbray, Alcock was faced with the either having a load of pies he could not sell or laying his staff off for a few days. What Alcock needed, and what he set out to get, was a new market for his pies.

Alcock therefore went to see Burbridge, who was responsible for managing the fast postal stagecoaches that changed horses at the George Hotel in High Street. What Alcock wanted to know was how to arrange for his surplus pies to be taken to London where they could surely be sold. Burbridge introduced Alcock to the nameless coach guard and together the three men struck a deal. The guard undertook to carry the surplus pies to a butcher he knew in London, sell them and bring the cash back to Alcock, having deducted a percentage for his services.

The first shipment of Alcock's Melton Mowbray pork pies went south on a horse-drawn stagecoach in the summer of 1831. Those huntsmen who came from London pounced on the chance to buy their favourite pies at home in London. The pies sold quickly and soon Alcock had expanded his business to produce enough pies to satisfy the London market. Then he thought about all those other towns and cities in England from which came men to hunt around Melton Mowbray. Might not there be a market in those towns as well? There was. Production and consumption boomed.

In 1840 a baker named Enoch Evans followed Alcock's lead and went into large scale production of the Melton Mowbray pork pie for export out of the town. Seven years later the railway system got to Syston, close enough for the station there to act as a shipment station for pork pies from Melton Mowbray. Production boomed again, and other bakers eagerly swelled the ranks of large-scale production. William Whalley, Henry Roberts, Elizabeth Short, John Dickinson (grandson of the inventor of the dolly) and Edward Basse all joined the trade.

But by the 1880s there was a problem. A large scale commercial baker in Leicester had begun making what he called 'Melton Mowbray pork pies' and selling them around the country. The product was not really up to the qualities of the pies being produced in the real town itself. The meat was minced, the crust thin and the resulting product not only inferior in taste, but entirely unable to be carried around in a pocket without falling to pieces. The manufacturers in Melton Mowbray conferred and decided to contest the Leicester baker's right to use the name of their town under copyright legislation. The court case failed. The judge ruled that any of the manufacturer's were free to copyright the name of their company, but that they could not collectively copyright the name of the town. Bakers across the country were free to produce inferior pies and call them 'Melton Mowbray'. All the town's bakers could do was display prominently on their packaging the proud boast that the pie within had been made in the town to the traditional recipe.

Despite this setback, the town's pie bakers flourished. The year 1887 saw the Gold Jubilee of Queen Victoria. The pie makers produced a range of celebratory products that encouraged consumption and boosted production. In the two weeks running up to the actual jubilee date itself, the town produced an astonishing total of twelve tons of pies. With this success under their belt, the bakers decided to cash in on the growing commercialisation of Christmas. Having a Melton Mowbray pork pie in the house to carve at over the Christmas season was promoted as being the true sign of a respectable family and generous host. The ploy worked and by 1900, the December surge in production was seeing over 150,000 pies leaving the town each festive season.

The railway station at Melton Mowbray. The arrival of the railway in the mid-nineteenth century enabled the town's pie makers to export their wares in greater quantities than ever before.

A range of the products made by Dickinson & Morris, including Melton Mowbray pork pies of various sizes and a plate of Leicestershire sausages.

In 1890 the pies hit the international trade. Cargo ships were by then being built with large refrigerated holds to transport quality meat – mostly lamb and mutton – from Australia and New Zealand to Britain. The idea was soon taken up by the beef merchants of North America, greatly boosting the demand for beef raised by cowboys in the Wild West. But the refrigerated ships needed some perishable product to take back again if they were to turn a profit. What better than a consignment of Melton Mowbray pork pies, or so thought the company of Evans & Hill. They packed up a crate of pies for chilling and sent them off to Borneo. It was the start of a highly profitable export trade.

But even as the pie bakers of Melton Mowbray were enjoying their boom years, the very basis of their trade was being undermined. The problem was two-fold. Firstly, the numbers of inferior pies being produced outside the town was increasing. This led the public to mistrust the label 'Melton Mowbray' as being synonymous with quality. No longer did buyers in shops across England gravitate toward a Melton Mowbray label when they wanted the best pork pie on offer.

Secondly, and most invidiously, the internal combustion engine had been invented. Motor cars and bikes remained inefficient and unreliable playthings of the rich until after the First World War. By 1920, however, motorised transport had become significantly more reliable, and it was becoming cheaper. A car was still out of the financial reach of most people, but increasingly doctors, lawyers, gentlemen and noblemen were coming to rely on their motor car to get them about. The process accelerated in the 1930s and by 1939 almost anyone who needed private transport – most people relied on public transport at this date – had abandoned a horse or horse and carriage in favour of a motor car.

Riding a horse was becoming what it is today, a sport. No longer did the dashing young A-listers and aspiring gentry desperate to show off their horses and horsemanship go hunting. Instead they took their motor cars down to Brighton for the weekend or drove off to have lunch at 'roadhouses', smart pubs and restaurants that dotted the main roads near large towns. There they would meet with other wealthy young types to show off their cars, talk about engine capacity and top speeds or simply to chat with like-minded fashionable folk and hope to catch the eye of the young ladies who also flocked to such places.

Melton Mowbray remained a key pivot in the world of foxhunting, but that sport was increasingly confined to country types or to those townsfolk who still liked to ride as a hobby. Because the younger, smarter set from towns were no longer going to Melton Mowbray in large numbers, they were no longer able to enjoy the delights of the genuine pie in its home town. They no longer went home to tell their friends about the fantastic pies on offer. They no longer demanded a genuine Melton Mowbray pork pie to be served at their tables in place of whatever the local baker could turn out.

By the 1930s, sales were falling, but not catastrophically so. The real crisis in Melton Mowbray pork pie production came with the Second World War. Not only was meat rationed, but the pork pie itself became what was known as a controlled food due to its high meat content. Production declined, companies closed down, bakehouses were shut. When peace came in 1945, rationing was not ended, that took several more years. The pie makers of Melton Mowbray were simply not equipped to regain their lost production or their lost reputations.

By 1955 only a few local bakers were still making Melton Mowbray pork pies the way they should be made. Fifteen years later there was only one: Dickinson & Morris based in Ye Olde Pork Pie Shoppe in Nottingham Street. Even they eked out an existence as general bakers with the once great pie being only one among many products.

**Left:** Melton Mowbray pork pies are made from uncured, prime cuts of pork and therefore have a greyish tinge to the contents. Many other sorts of pork pie are made using cured meat and therefore have a pinkish hue to the meat contents.

**Right:** The heart of the Melton Mowbray pork pie business lies here in Ye Olde Pork Pie Shoppe, home to Dickinson & Morris, the oldest of the companies making the 'King of Pies' in this Leicestershire town.

And then a revival began. Perversely it was the large, mass production bakers making 'Melton Mowbray' pies many miles away from the town that began the process. They began using the town's name as a designation of the premier pies in their range. These were not traditional pies as they had been baked in the town, but they were the top quality products of the age. The heavy marketing budgets of these huge companies was brought to bear on the pork pie market, promoting the Melton Mowbray name to encourage customers to spend more on a quality product.

Stephen Hallam of Dickinson & Morris displays a fine tray of Melton Mowbray Pork Pies made by his company outside the firm's shop in the centre of the town.

That sparked interest in the genuine article. Before long newspaper, columnists and chefs were beginning to investigate the history of the Melton Mowbray pork pie and, crucially, its availability. As the only company then making the traditional pie, it was Dickinson & Morris who benefited most from this renewed interest. Their sales began to climb. Once again pies began to be exported from the town in numbers. This time it was to supermarket shelves that the pies went.

Inevitably as the market for genuine Melton Mowbray pork pies increased, others were encouraged to enter production. Soon other bakers and butchers began to produce pork pies in the traditional fashion. Each had its own variant on the exact blend of herbs to be included, and each had its own band of dedicated admirers. By the 1990s things were almost back to the state of the 1880s. The pies were a major local product making an important contribution to the local economy.

And then an old problem raised its head. Bakers from miles away began making imitation pies and naming them Melton Mowbray. Some of these pies were, it must be admitted, pretty good and some were even made in the traditional fashion, but many of them were inferior. The pie makers of Melton Mowbray did not want to see their trade suffer the way it had done before. Copyright law had not changed, but food laws had.

The new band of Melton Mowbray pork pie makers based in and around the town began a new legal battle. The seven producers then in operation formed the Melton Mowbray Pork Pie Association in 1998 with the aim of gaining Protected Geographical Indication (PGI) status for the Melton Mowbray pork pie from the Commission of the European Union.

This PGI gives legal protection for named regional food products against imitation across the EU. It aims to protect and promote regional food products, the consumer interest and rural economies against national and international supply chains. It seeks to encourage diverse agricultural production, protect product names from misuse and imitation and to help consumers by giving them information about the specific character of the products concerned. It stops manufacturers from outside a region from copying a regional product and selling it as if it were that regional product. PGI is available for products that originated in that region and which are either produced or processed or prepared in a geographical area. It is available only to food products where the specific quality, reputation or other characteristics of the product are due to the area from which it comes.

The Association worked hard for several years to gain PGI status for the Melton Mowbray pork pie, as this would protect the integrity of the Melton Mowbray pork pie and resist its denigration at the hands of manufacturers outside the Melton area, thereby ensuring its survival and stop the consumer from being misled about the provenance and quality of Melton Mowbray pork pies. It would, of course, also promote the Melton Mowbray pork pie so that as many people as possible are able to try this famous regional food, encourage growth and investment in the rural economy, protect the good name of the town of Melton Mowbray and therefore boost its important tourist economy – all of which was of great benefit to the town and region.

In October 2008 the EU Commission announced that Melton Mowbray pork pies would be granted the coveted PGI status, joining thirty-four other British products such as Arbroath Smokies, Cornish Clotted Cream, Welsh Lamb and Scottish Farmed Salmon. As a protected product, Melton Mowbray pork pies can now only be labelled as such if they are made using the correct ingredients in the traditional manner and in a designated area around the town.

The new designation recognised that the Melton Mowbray pork pie of the twenty-first century is a distinct product that is recognisably different from other pork pies, both in physical characteristics and in reputation. It is rich in history and is recognised by consumers as a traditional, regional food product.

The sides of the Melton Mowbray pork pie are bow-shaped as they are baked free standing, whereas most other pork pies are straight-sided, being baked in hoops. The meat used is fresh pork which is naturally grey when cooked (like roast pork), not pink like most other pork pies, which use cured pork. The meat must be pure chopped pork, not minced pork. The Melton Mowbray pork pie is also well jellied and the meat seasoned with salt and pepper.

In 2009 there were ten members of the Melton Mowbray Pork Pie Association:

**F Bailey & Son**
Station Road
Upper Broughton
Melton Mowbray
Leicestershire
LE14 3BQ
Tel: 01664 822216

**Brockleby's Farm Shop**
The Grange
Asfordby Hill
Melton Mowbray
Leicetsershire
LE14 3QU
Tel: 01664 813200
www.brocklebys.co.uk

**Chappell's Fine Foods**
61 Chartswell Drive
Wigston
Leicester
LE18 2FS
Tel: 0116 2812087
www.meltonmowbrayporkpies.com

**Dickinson & Morris**
Ye Olde Pork Pie Shoppe
8–10 Nottingham Street
Melton Mowbray
Leicestershire
LE4 1ZN
Tel: 01664 562341
www.porkpie.co.uk

**Mrs Elizabeth King Ltd**
Unit 30
High Hazles Road
Cotgrave
Nottingham
NG12 3GZ
Tel: 0115 9894101

**Nelsons of Stamford**
Alma Place
North Street
Stamford
Lincolnshire
PE9 1EG
Tel: 01780 763345
www.nelsonsbutchers.co.uk

**Northfield Farm**
Whissendine Lane
Cold Overton
Oakham
Rutland
LE15 7QF
Tel: 01664 474271
www.northfieldfarm.com

**Patricks**
85 Sibson Road
Birstall
Leicester
LE4 4NB
Tel: 0116 2674341
www.markpatrickbutchers.co.uk

**Pork Farms Ltd**
Queens Drive
Nottingham
NG2 1LU
Tel: 0115 866541
www.pork-farms.co.uk

**Walkers (Charnwood) Bakery**
200 Madeline Road
Beaumont Leys
Leicester
LE4 1EX
Tel: 0116 2344500
www.samworthbrothers.co.uk

*Five*

# FROM THE DAIRY

Anyone wanting a quick snack could do a lot worse than cut themselves a chunk of cheese to eat with a slice of tasty bread and, perhaps, some pickle. It is a classic combination that in England has for many years gone by the name of a ploughman's lunch – though the ingredients work equally well in the form of a sandwich. With some lush grazing ground on the wetter areas of clay soil, Leicestershire has long been a prime county for grazing livestock, and milk is a major product of the dairy industry.

The oldest sign of cheesemaking in Leicestershire comes in the form of a broken piece of pottery with a hole in it that has been dated to around 500 BC. The misshapen lump of broken pot does not look like much, and if it were not for the fact that archaeologists have more complete examples from elsewhere with which to compare it, the object might have remained a mystery. What this find was before it was broken and thrown away was almost certainly a cheesewring. This device looks rather like a wide-bottomed casserole dish with holes drilled into its base. It is used to separate the curds from the whey, one of the key processes in the making of cheese.

The original reason why milk was turned into cheese is the same as that for the production of butter - food preservation. In the days when most of the population in Leicestershire were subsistence farmers, famine and death through starvation were permanent worries. In a county as lush as Leicestershire, famine did not strike often – perhaps only once in a lifetime – but it was a big killer and a major risk. Nobody knew when a sudden dry spell or torrential downpour might ruin a crop, nor when a disease might sweep through the ranks of livestock and

A cow suckles its calf on the farm where Sparkenhoe Red Leicester cheese is made. The calves are allowed to feed naturally for some time, but once they have weaned, the cow continues to give milk that is then taken for conversion into cheese.

wipe them out. In such an unpredictable world it was essential to keep and store as much food as possible. Then if one crop failed, there was something to fall back on.

Milking livestock – be it cows, ewes or goats – has always produced a good source of energy, vitamins and minerals. Milk is one of the great foods available to mankind, but it is flawed by the fact that it goes off very quickly. Milk simply cannot be stored by putting it in jars or pots and being left on the shelf. It would become inedible within days – or hours on a really hot day. Before the days of fridges, freezers or food driers, some other way had to be found to preserve the goodness of milk for possibly leaner days in the future.

The simplest method was to turn it into butter. The basic method was known way back in prehistory. Milk is put into a container of wood or pottery which can be kept at a steady temperature – not much of a problem in summer but more of a challenge in winter. The container is then repeatedly shaken or agitated. Some containers were mounted on pivots and turned by a handle, others had a paddle inserted into them that could be turned, while still others were mounted on rockers to be nudged back and forth.

As the milk was shaken about, the individual fat particles got stuck together into globules that floated to the top of the liquid. The fat could then be sieved out, spread out to dry and finally packed into large pottery jars that were then stopped with an airtight seal. In this form, butter would keep for weeks, enabling a sudden glut of milk to be stored for consumption later.

Among the Coritani, the Celtic tribe that inhabited the eastern Midlands before the Romans came, butter was reckoned to be a luxury food. In normal times it was used only at special feasts, or served to show that the host was conferring special honour on to a guest. The nobles loved it, and consumed it in great quantities.

Alongside butter, the earliest farmers probably made a form of cream cheese. This is also easy to produce; all that is needed is for milk to be left in an open dish for bacteria to curdle it. Obviously the right sort of bacteria are needed, or the milk would simply go off. The Celts of more than 2,000 years ago did not know that bacteria existed, but they were intelligent human beings with a vast wealth of experience. They would soon have learned that a dish in which milk had curdled once would reliably make milk curdle again – so long as it was not washed out. The bacteria from one batch was able to survive on the clay walls of the dish long enough to start work on the next. The curds resulting from this process were drained, formed into small round patties and laid out to dry. They were often flavoured with chopped herbs.

Exactly when somebody had the bright idea of using rennet to curdle milk in place of bacteria in pots is unclear. It was certainly being used by around 100 BC. Rennet is a chemical that can be extracted from the stomach of sheep, goats or cattle, though a similar chemical found in thistles will work just as well. Usually a small piece of animal stomach was dropped into the milk to start the process.

The importance of rennet in the making of cheese is that it relies on different enzymes to curdle the milk. These chemicals not only produce a slightly different composition of curds and whey, but also continue to work on the curds allowing cheese to ripen and mature once it has been made.

Of course, it was not always possible to slaughter an animal when a glut of milk appeared, so most farming families took to storing the stomach linings, which caused the milk to curdle. There were two ways to do this. First the stomach lining could be dried, and then hung up in a chimney to smoke. Alternatively, it could be filled with milk curd and stored in a sealed tub of salted water. Either way the potential for contamination of the stomach lining by bacteria and other infective

The team that makes Sparkenhoe Red Leicester cheese together with a calf and some of their produce outside the farmhouse. Sparkenhoe is the only craft-made Red Leicester cheese that is actually produced in Leicestershire.

agents was high. Some of this contamination spoiled the cheese, but other contaminants merely gave the cheese an unusual flavour – sometimes a very attractive flavour indeed.

During the centuries after the fall of Rome, Leicestershire lay on a dramatic cusp when it came to livestock keeping. Most of the lands to the south and east saw sheep kept in large numbers for wool and milk. Such cattle as were kept served as draught animals. On the hills to the north, people tended to keep cattle in larger numbers for both meat and milk. It would seem that before about 1400 Leicestershire had more sheep than cattle, but after that date the numbers of cattle increased steadily and greatly as more of the wetter, lowland clays were cleared of forest and put over to summer pasture.

Around 1550 or so, farmers in Leicestershire stopped milking ewes. By this date the money to be made from sheep came from their wool and there was a great pressure to keep sheep over winter. If ewes had been artificially forced to put their energies into providing milk by regular milking after the lambs had been weaned, then they were weaker come the chills of autumn and less likely to survive the winter. Quite simply the farmers could earn more money by not milking their sheep than by milking them. Ewe's milk fell out of use and its place in Leicestershire was taken by cow's milk by around 1650.

One property of cow's milk was that it was possible to make cheese from the buttermilk left over after butter had been churned. This cheese came out very hard and was not much liked by richer folk. It was, however, a staple in the diet of poorer people. Much ingenuity went into making these hard cheeses palatable. Most often this involved grating them up and using them in cooked dishes, but some dairy workers tried various methods by which buttermilk cheese could be made that was not hard enough to blunt a knife.

A half wheel of Sparkenhoe Red Leicester cheese. The cheese was always traditionally made in this shape, which allows for even maturing of the cheese and the formation of the characteristic slightly crumbly texture.

David Clarke shows off some of his award winning Sparkenhoe Red Leicester cheese. He and his wife have successfully re-established a craft dairy on their farm.

Coincidentally, or otherwise, the later seventeenth century saw the emergence of cheesemongers. The first city to establish a guild of cheesemongers was London in the 1680s, but other towns and cities soon followed suit and Leicester had an informal cheesemongers association by 1710. In the larger cities, the aim of the cheesemongers was to source good, reliable supplies of cheese that they could buy in wholesale, then sell on retail. For the smaller towns, of which Leicester was one, the aim was as much to ship out cheeses to the larger cities as it was to sell it retail to the citizens. As we shall see in the chapter on Stilton cheese, they sought out novel or unusual cheeses with which to tempt their clients.

At about the same time there was a growing fashion for colouring cheeses. Marigold petal juice, beetroot juice, carrot juice and other vegetable or fruit juices were mixed in with the curds before they were pressed into cheeses for maturing. These became especially popular if made into a cheese sauce to be served over a white vegetable such as leeks or cauliflower. By the end of the century the fashion for this type of artificially coloured cheese was over and most English cheesemakers abandoned the practice, with one major exception - Leicestershire.

In Leicestershire, for reasons that are not at all clear, most farmers' wives and dairy workers continued with the practice of adding vegetable juices to cheeses early in the manufacturing process. At this date they were turning out cheeses in a variety of different colours, but Red Leicester soon established itself as the most popular. At this date the colouring used was very much a matter of taste and varied from farm to farm. Carrot and beetroot juice seem to have been the most popular.

In the course of the 1850s, a novel method of making cheese in large quantities began to spread across England by word of mouth. The key innovations had been developed by Thomas Harding of Somerset, the son of a dairy farming family of some generations' experience. Harding's key maxim was that 'cheese is not made in the field, nor in the byre, but in the dairy.' He believed that it was what the cheesemaker did in the dairy itself that determined the type of cheese that came out at the end of the process. Earlier cheesemakers had thought that the breed of cow from which the milk had come and where it had grazed was equally important.

Harding insisted on absolute cleanliness in his dairy at all times. Every person entering the dairy – and access was strictly controlled – had to wash their hands and take off any soiled clothes. All cheesemaking equipment was cleaned thoroughly between batches. He also invented a cheese mill which drained curds more by stirring them and breaking them up than by squeezing them in the old cheese press.

The cheese that Harding produced and which he made on his farm to enormous profit was Cheddar. But his methods were quickly adapted in other areas where they hastened a move away from farm-based dairies and toward more commercial operations which brought milk in from several farms to be turned into cheese.

In Leicestershire, the introduction of the Harding methods led to two changes in how Red Leicester was produced. First the variety of vegetable juices were dropped in favour of an imported food colouring called annato, now known technically as E160b. This is a plant extract from South America made from the seed pods of the achiote tree. This produces a more reliably orangey colour than vegetable juices, and also imparts a slightly peppery flavour.

The second change saw a subtle alteration in the texture of the cheese. Instead of being crumbly and flaky, the cheese became smoother, though it still retained a slight tendency to crumble and was nowhere near as smooth as Cheddar.

The Gopsall Farm ice cream trailer travels around events in Leicestershire during the summer, taking the many delicious varieties of their homemade ice cream and sorbet to the hungry folk of the county.

A passing stall holder stops to enjoy a taster of Gopsall Farm vanilla ice cream at a fair held in the summer of 2008.

The Victorian period saw a fashion for serving cheese boards with several identifiably different types of cheese on it. The aim was to make the cheese as visually attractive and varied as possible. Mrs Beeton, in her seminal book on running a household, differentiated between how cheese was served in the 1860s 'at good tables' and in more humble homes. 'The usual mode of serving cheese at good tables,' Mrs Beeton wrote, 'is to cut a small quantity of each cheese into neat square pieces, and to put them into a glass cheese dish, this dish being handed round.' For other tables 'it may be put on the table in one piece, and the host may cut from it. When served thus, the cheese must always be carefully scraped and laid on a white 'doyley or napkin, neatly folded.' She concluded by observing that 'cucumber or watercress should always form part of a cheese course', presumably to add a touch of green colour to the dish.

With its red colour, reliable supply and slightly crumbly texture, Red Leicester cheese proved to be a major success in the later nineteenth century. With this success came an increase in demand. Perhaps because the Red Leicester cheese was being made by a number of large dairy companies, there was a gradual change in the way it was produced. By the 1950s the cheese that was usually sold as being Red Leicester was, in fact, identical to a mild Cheddar which had had some annato added to it. Such is still the case today.

There are a few craft dairies which still produce Red Leicester as it was made in the nineteenth century, selling a cheese that is slightly crumbling and has a nutty or peppery flavour. These cheeses are produced in the traditional wheel shape and matured in cloth for between six and nine months. Only two such dairies are to be found in Leicestershire itself: Long Clawson Dairy and Sparkenhoe Farm, though a third, Quenby Hall, has plans to start production in 2009. The three dairies have begun a campaign to have the name 'Leicestershire Cheese' reserved for their craft-made product, while mass produced red cheese from other parts of the UK would still be known as 'Red Leicester'.

# Leicestershire Fish Roll

| Serves 6 | Preparation time: 30 minutes | Cooking time: 15 minutes |
|---|---|---|

This cracking starter packs a tasty punch. It goes well before a robust main dish, such as stewed beef or game.

## Ingredients

6 crusty white bread rolls
12oz cooked white fish (cod, haddock etc), flaked
½pt white sauce
3oz Red Leicester cheese, grated
1 tablespoon cream
Salt and pepper.

## Method

❖ Start by slicing the end off each roll and removing the soft bread from within to leave only the hard crust.
❖ In a bowl, mix the flaked fish, white sauce, grated cheese, cream and salt and pepper.
❖ Spoon the mixture into the empty bread rolls and replace the tops.
❖ Bake in a moderate oven (180°C Gas Mk 4) for 15 minutes.

Note: The leftover bread can be turned into bread crumbs for use in other recipes. This may be stored in a freezer if sealed tightly in a plastic bag.

# Leicestershire Toasties

| Serves 4 | Preparation time: 10 minutes | Cooking time: 5 minutes |

This quick and tasty snack was developed as a breakfast dish to use up leftovers from dinner the night before. Modern palates might find this a bit rich for breakfast, so maybe it should be served for lunch. Either way, it is a smashing dish and a meal in itself.

## Ingredients

4 slices of bread, the thicker the better
Leftover wine or beer
6oz Red Leicester cheese, grated
1teaspoon English mustard
Milk

## Method

❖ Soak the slices of bread in the wine or beer until it has soaked up the liquid.

❖ Meanwhile, mix the grated cheese with the mustard and a little milk.

❖ Place the damp bread on to a grill pan and gently toast one side.

❖ Turn the bread over and lightly toast again.

❖ Spread the cheese mixture over the bread.

❖ Return to the grill and cook until the cheese bubbles.

# Cheesy Mushrooms

| Serves 6 | Preparation time: 25 minutes | Cooking time: 30 minutes |

Another lovely starter, this dish will not overpower a main course of fish or chicken and is probably best served before one of these more delicate meats rather than before game or beef. It will also make a tasty lunchtime snack.

## Ingredients

6 large, flat mushrooms
½oz butter
1 small onion, peeled and finely chopped
1 tablespoon breadcrumbs
2oz Red Leicester cheese, grated
Salt and pepper
6 slices of thin white bread

## Method

❖ Wash the mushrooms and lay on a greased baking tray.

❖ In a pan gently fry the onions in the butter until translucent, but not browned.

❖ In a bowl, mix together the breadcrumbs, grated cheese and salt and pepper.

❖ Add the cooked onions and butter to the cheese mixture, mix thoroughly.

❖ Spoon the mixture on to the mushrooms and press gently to shape it into domes.

❖ Place the mushrooms into a hot oven (200°C/Gas Mark 6) for 30 minutes.

❖ Just before the mushrooms are ready, toast the slices of bread.

❖ Place a slice of bread on each plate, topped by a steaming hot mushroom fresh from the oven.

# Mackerel with Red Leicester

**Serves 4**  **Preparation time: 5 minutes**  **Cooking time: 8 minutes**

Mackerel is one of the most underrated fish to be found in British waters. It is firm, meaty and has a delicious, rather robust flavour. It is also easy to fillet and has fewer small bones to annoy the diner than many other types of fish. For this recipe it is best to start with mackerel fillets, which any decent fishmonger will produce and which can be found in most supermarkets.

## Ingredients

2 mackerel, filleted into 4 portions x 200g (7oz)
4oz Red Leicester cheese, thinly sliced
salt and pepper

## Method

❖ Place the fish on a grill pan and grill at a high heat for 8 minutes, turning once.
❖ Remove the fish from the grill and turn again.
❖ Top each fillet with slices of cheese.
❖ Grill again for about 30 seconds, or until the cheese just begins to melt.
❖ Serve piping hot.


# Leicester Cheesy Yachts

**Serves 4**  **Preparation time: 10 minutes**  **Cooking time: 50 minutes**

We all like a bit of fun with our food from time to time, especially the children amongst us. You could try this dish next time your child (if you have one) brings a pal home from school. Otherwise enjoy it yourself – it is yummy and easy to prepare. Have some Worcestershire sauce on the table for those (such as me) who like it.

## Ingredients

4 large potatoes, suitable for baking
8oz Red Leicester cheese
8 cocktail sticks

## Method

❖ Prick the potatoes and place on a baking tray.
❖ Bake in a hot oven (200°C/Gas Mark 6) for 50 minutes (time may vary depending on size of potatoes).
❖ Meanwhile, cut the cheese into slices. Then cut each slice into 2 triangles. You will probably cause some waste as the cheese may crumble, but don't worry. Put any 'failed' slices into a bowl and crumble it up completely.
❖ When the potatoes are cooked, remove from the oven and slice in half.
❖ Put two halves skin side down on each plate and sprinkle the crumbled cheese over them.
❖ Stick a cocktail stick into each potato half to form a 'mast'.
❖ Lean a triangle of cheese against each 'mast' to form a 'sail'.
❖ Serve at once before the heat from the potatoes melts the base of the cheese 'sail' and causes it to fall over.

# Fruit-Cheese Salad

| Serves 4 | Preparation time: 20 minutes | Cooking time: nil. |
|---|---|---|

This light dish is inspired by the Victorian craze for mixing cheeses of different colours, but also nods to the New York dish of Waldorf Salad to create a light, healthy lunchtime meal.

## Ingredients

4oz Red Leicester cheese
4oz mature Cheddar cheese
4oz Sage Derby cheese
Juice of 1 lemon
6 sticks of celery, cut into ½ inch chunks
2 red apples, cored and chopped
6oz red seedless grapes, halved if large but otherwise left whole
1 iceberg lettuce, finely sliced or shredded

## Method

❖ Cut all the cheese into ½ inch cubes and mix.
❖ Place all the ingredients into a large bowl and mix lightly until thoroughly mixed together.
❖ Serve with thinly sliced white bread and butter.

# Leicester Cheese Pie

| Serves 8 | Preparation time: 20 minutes | Cooking time: 1 hour |
|---|---|---|

This is a great way to use Red Leicester cheese. The final dish comes out of the oven beautifully browned and releases the most wonderful aroma when it is cut open. I like to have some Worcestershire sauce on the table for this and slap it over liberally.

## Ingredients

1lb shortcrust pastry
1lb Red Leicester cheese, grated
1 small onion, chopped
2 tomatoes, chopped
2 teaspoon English mustard
3 eggs, beaten
Salt and pepper
A little milk

## Method

❖ Roll out ⅔ of the pastry to line the base and sides of an 8 inch pie dish.
❖ In a bowl mix the grated cheese, onion, beaten eggs, chopped tomatoes, mustard and salt and pepper.
❖ When it is completely mixed, pile the mixture into the pie case.
❖ Roll out the remaining pastry into a circle large enough to form the lid.
❖ Place the lid on to the pie, using milk to get a good seal.
❖ Cut a small hole in the top of the pie lid to allow steam to escape.
❖ Brush the pie lid with a little milk.
❖ Bake in a moderate oven (180°C/Gas Mark 4) for an hour.

*six*

# STILTON – THE 'QUEEN OF CHEESES'

Stilton cheese is a magnificent food – tasty, fragrant, filling and so versatile that it can be used in a countless multitude of dishes. Stilton actually comes in two varieties. The best known is Blue Stilton, but the creamy and rather milder White Stilton is also a cheese of distinction.

The origins of the mighty Blue Stilton are much debated and the subject of some controversy. Different villages in Leicestershire lay claim to the honour of inventing the cheese, but most authorities are agreed that there are two main contenders, Wymondham and Little Dalby.

To take the claims of Little Dalby first. Sometime around 1710 a farmer's wife named Mrs Orton was living in Church Lane, Little Dalby. She found that one batch of her cheese had 'gone wrong' and had turned out quite unlike any cheese that she had ever seen. Instead of being creamily white and smooth when cut open, the cheese had a crumbly texture and had veins of blue mould running through it. Fortunately, Mrs Orton decided to taste her 'gone wrong' cheese before consigning it to animal feed. She found that the cheese had a powerful and extremely pleasant new flavour.

Mrs Orton tried the cheese out on her neighbours, and they loved it too. Her next task was to try to replicate what had 'gone wrong' with that first batch of cheese in order to make another similar batch. At this early date the science behind cheese manufacture was quite unknown. We now know that the blue veining is caused by a fungus known as *Penicillium roqueforti*. Modern manufacturers carefully introduce the spores of the fungus during the making of the cheese.

But Mrs Orton had no way of knowing what was affecting her cheese. She came to believe that it was some special quality in the turf of her main cow grazing field, known as Orton's Close, that was responsible for the new type of cheese. She carefully kept her cows in Orton's Close for the days when they were being milked for the next batch of cheese. Lo and behold, the next batch came out blue as well. In fact, it was microscopic traces of the fungus sticking to her cheesemaking equipment that was doing the trick.

Mrs Orton's neighbours came to wonder at the new cheese and to eat it in some quantity. Soon Mrs Orton's cheese was selling well in nearby markets and she was shifting every cheese that she could make. Keen to increase production, she began keeping more cattle, grazing them on her prized Orton's Close in rotation. Nearby dairies wanted to get in on the act to make the top selling cheese. Quite how they managed it is unclear. One old story says that they came at night to cut turfs from Orton's Close and plant it in their own fields so that the magic grass

Church Lane in Little Dalby. According to local stories, Stilton cheese was developed by a Mrs Orton who lived here from about 1680 to around 1720.

would spread and grow. Since it was not the grass that made the blue cheese blue, this cannot be how the secret spread – though that is not to say that nocturnal turf stealing did not take place. More likely is the theory that they came to talk to Mrs Orton and inadvertently got spores of the fungus onto their clothes, which then transferred to their own dairies.

The claims of Wymondham are better documented, but not as old. Those who uphold the Wymondham version pour scorn on the stories about Mrs Orton at Little Dalby. There were, they say, dozens of blue cheeses were being made by farmers' wives across the county. Each cheese was different, each was tasty, but none of them was anything like the modern Stilton. Mrs Orton, the Wymondham folk say, was just one of many.

The key figure in the Wymondham version of events is Frances Pawlett, who was born at Sproxton in 1720 but moved to Wymondham when she married her second husband, William Pawlett, in 1742. Like all good farm girls, Frances had learned how to make cheese from her mother. Her new husband was a relatively wealthy farmer who owned his own land and, crucially, ran a small commercial dairy making butter, cheese and other products for sale in nearby towns.

Frances took over the running of the dairy and decided to put the production of cheese on to a sound, standardised footing. She did away with the rough and ready techniques used up until then, brought in standardised equipment and insisted on cleanliness and diligence in her workers. The Pawlett dairy was soon turning out blue cheeses of a high and consistent quality. It was the blue cheese we now know as Stilton, but the name was yet to be given to it.

One of the Pawlett cheeses was bought by an innkeeper named Cooper Thornhill, who owned and ran the Bell Inn in the village of Stilton, over the county border in Cambridgeshire. Stilton has now been bypassed by the modern dual-carriageway that today forms the A1, but in 1744 when Thornhill bought Mrs Pawlett's cheese, it was on the main London to York highway. Stilton was one of the main staging villages, meaning that it was here that the horses were changed and passengers made a brief stop to refresh themselves. The Bell Inn was one of the more important and grander of the inns that catered to the vast numbers of coach passengers.

It was one of those passengers, who was so taken by the blue cheese that he was served, that asked Thornhill if he could buy a whole cheese to take with him. That gave Thornhill the idea of selling not just snacks and meals, but cheeses as well. He sent off for a large order from Frances Pawlett, then put the whole cheeses on sale at his inn. They were snapped up, so he ordered more and then even more. Within a few years it was not just coach passengers who bought the cheeses that by then were known as Stilton, but cheesemongers from every major city in Britain.

The success of the Stilton cheese was boosted by the fame of Thornhill as a great 'character' of the age – we would use the word 'celebrity' today. He had taken over the Bell in 1730 and set out to make it and himself as well known as possible. He famously staged riding exploits designed to pack the customers in to his inn. The most famous of these took place on 29 April 1745 after a heated discussion in the Bell had taken place about how fast a man could ride from the Bell to Shoreditch Church in the City of London.

Thornhill boasted that he could ride from the Bell to Shoreditch, back to the Bell and then back to Shoreditch again in the hours of daylight. The assembled horsemen refused to believe him, so Thornhill began taking bets. In all he staked 500 guineas, then a huge sum of money, on his success. Thornhill set about the task with grim determination and great skill. He arranged for nineteen horses to be stationed along the Great North Road, each one saddled and waiting

The Bell Inn at Stilton. It was the colourful innkeeper Cooper Thornhill who first sold Stilton cheese here to passengers on the passing stagecoaches. Thornhill staged a number of exciting publicity stunts to publicise his inn and the cheese that it sold.

The Great North Road at Stilton. The Bell Inn where Stilton cheese was first sold is on the right. The village is now bypassed by the A1 but in the days of horse travel, this was the main north-south highway from London to York. The street outside the Bell was made wide enough to allow a coach and four horses to turn around without the need for any backing up.

for him to leap on to it. Ostlers were on hand to take away the exhausted mount that Thornhill abandoned as he sprang to the new one.

Then Thornhill set about publicising the bet and the date of his attempt. Thousands of people flocked to Stilton and to Shoreditch, while thousands more found a place to stand along the Great North Road to watch him pass. The stagecoach companies made a fortune transporting spectators and happily agreed to clear the road for Thornhill on the day itself.

By the time Thornhill came out of the Bell and mounted his horse in the street outside at 4 a.m., the street was thronged with over a thousand people. Ever the businessman, Thornhill had previously made certain that his inn was packed with food and drink to sell to the crowd while they awaited his return. As Thornhill sat on his horse the judges anxiously scanned the eastern sky for the first sign of sunlight, long before the sun itself came up over the horizon. At 4.15 a.m. they gave the signal and Thornhill set off.

Riding all the way at the gallop, Thornhill covered the 213 miles up and down the Great North Road in twelve hours. As he tore into Shoreditch at 4 p.m. that afternoon he was cheered in by a crowd estimated at over 4,000. Exhausted, but triumphant, Thornhill pocketed the 500 guineas. Next day he rode back to Stilton to count his profits on the day's trading.

The rapidly growing demand for Stilton cheeses led to a boom in production. The Pawlett's were very soon in partnership with Thornhill, producing and marketing Stilton cheese throughout the country by means of the stagecoaches which called in at Stilton village. Mrs Pawlett died in 1808 after a long, eventful and prosperous career. For some reason her gravestone records her age as being ninety, though the church records would make her only eighty-eight. It was a great age for the time at any rate.

An armchair nestles beside the fireplace in the front room of the older part of the Bell Inn. It was here that Cooper Thornhill used to entertain his favourite or most honoured customers.

By the time Mrs Pawlett died, Stilton cheese was being made on almost every farm that kept cows in eastern Leicestershire. It was being sold through a vast number of cheesemongers in towns and cities who had developed a complex network of distribution coach routes that ensured the cheeses got to the shops in good condition and well matured.

The boom in demand for the cheese meant more whey being produced as a by-product. Whey itself can make for a refreshing and wholesome drink, as the old nursery rhyme about Little Miss Muffet reminds us. It was especially popular in summer when it was taken from the cool, dark dairy to the men and women working in the fields to quench their thirsts and cool them down. But there was a limit to how much whey a person could drink, and in any case the farmers already knew of another very profitable use for the liquid. That was to boil it up with bran and feed it to pigs. The increase in spare whey meant that there was a glut of cheap pig food, which in turn led to an increase in the numbers of pigs. By happy coincidence this occurred at just the time that Melton Mowbray pork pies were becoming really popular, so there was a ready market for all the pork. The pies also created a demand for the flour to make the crusts and since the crusts were made of white flour, there was a surplus of bran and chaff being turned out by the local windmills. That bran and chaff was then fed to the pigs, producing even more pork.

By the early nineteenth century, there was a virtuous circle of production going on in eastern Leicestershire as the cheesemakers produced spare whey and the millers produced spare bran, both of which were fed to the pigs that were slaughtered for the pork pie trade. The economy of the area boomed as the rest of the country enjoyed the cheese and pies.

In 1840 the railways came to Leicestershire and very soon after that arrived refrigerated wagons. Stilton cheeses could now be transported further than ever before and still remain in good condition. The cheeses even began to be exported overseas in refrigerated ships.

In 1875 the first mass production dairy making Stilton cheese was opened by Thomas Nuttall at Beeby. He bought in milk from surrounding farms, processing it into Stilton and then took it to the market in Melton Mowbray where he sold it to the representatives of cheesemongers from

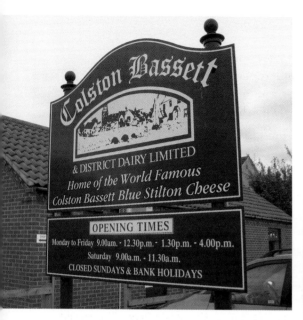

The Colston Bassett Dairy where Stilton cheese of the finest quality is made. The dairy sells small quantities of the cheese direct to the public from the small shop behind the sign.

The market cross in Melton Mowbray. During the late nineteenth century, special Cheese Fairs were organised here to cope with the vast quantities of Stilton cheese being traded through the town.

far and wide. Other local cheesemakers noticed Nuttall's success and within three years, several other industrial scale dairies had opened up. Among these was Webster's, the oldest of the dairies producing Stilton cheese into the twenty-first century.

In the autumn of 1883 the authorities running the market in Melton Mowbray realised that the increasing volume of cheeses arriving on market days was crowding out the older businesses. They set up a new Cheese Fair on different days where only cheese was to be sold, freeing up the market place for more traditional stall holders. By then Nuttall had expanded his business in two directions. He had both opened a new dairy in Melton Mowbray itself, but with rather more initiative he had set out to try to find an area where the grasslands matched the specific grazing qualities of the area around Wymondham and Melton Mowbray. He found it far to the north-west around Buxton, where a small section of Derbyshire produced grass that came up to his exacting standards.

In 1936 an organisation, The Stilton Cheesemakers' Association, was formed to maintain the quality standards and protect the name of Stilton. Unlike the makers of Melton Mowbray pork pies a generation earlier, they managed to have 'Stilton' registered as a trademark and set out exacting standards for cheese to be able to be sold as such.

The official rules state that to be called Stilton a cheese must:

- Have been made in a dairy licensed by The Stilton Cheesemakers' Association;
- Have been made in a dairy located in Derbyshire, Nottinghamshire or Leicestershire;
- Have been made from local milk that has been pasteurised;
- Have been made only in the traditional cylindrical shape;
- Have been allowed to form its own coat naturally;
- Have never been pressed and;
- Exhibit the famous and magical blue veining that is unique to Stilton.

Beyond the rules laid down by the association, all makers of Stilton cheese scrupulously follow a set pattern of production that ensures high quality cheese. Early each morning fresh milk is delivered to the dairy from local farms. There it is pasteurised and then fed into an open vat to which acid forming bacteria, a milk clotting agent and the famous fungus *penicillium roqueforti* are added. Once the curds have formed, the whey is drained off and the curds allowed to drain overnight. The following morning, the curd is cut into blocks to allow further drainage before being milled and salted.

Each cheese requires about 24lb of salted curd that is fed into cylindrical moulds. The moulds are then placed on boards and turned daily to allow natural drainage for five or six days. This ensures an even distribution of moisture throughout the cheese so that, as the cheese is never pressed, it creates the flaky, open texture required for the important blueing stage. After five or six days, the cylinders are removed and the coat of each cheese is sealed by smoothing or wrapping to prevent any air entering the inside of the cheese. The cheese is then transferred to the store where temperature and humidity are carefully controlled. Each cheese is turned regularly during this ripening period. At about six weeks, the cheese has begun to form the traditional Stilton crust and it is then ready for piercing with stainless steel needles. This allows air to enter the body of the cheese and create the magical blue veins associated with Stilton.

At about nine weeks of age, by which time each cheese now weighs about 17lbs, the cheese is ready to be sold. But before this happens, every cheese must be graded using a cheese iron. The iron is used to bore into the cheese and extract a plug of cheese. By visual inspection and by smell the grader can determine whether the cheese is up to the mark and able to be sold as Stilton. Cheese that is not up to the mark will be sold as 'blue cheese'.

At this age, Stilton is still quite crumbly and has a slightly acidic taste. Some customers prefer a more mature cheese and after a further five or six weeks it will have a smoother, almost buttery texture, with a more rounded, mellow flavour.

White Stilton is also a protected name cheese and is made in a similar way to its blue cousin – except that no mould spores are added and the cheese is usually sold at about four weeks of age. It is a crumbly, creamy, open textured cheese and is now extensively used as a base for blending with apricot, ginger and citrus or vine fruits to create unique dessert cheeses.

## Stages in the production of Stilton cheese

**1**. First the milk arrives at the dairy and is pasteurised to remove any impurities or traces of unwanted bacteria that may have entered it during the milking or transportation process. (photo by Noriko Maegawa)

**2**. After pasteurisation, the milk is poured into a large stainless steel vat that has been carefully sterilised to remove any contaminants. The special mould that will later form the blue veins and distinctive flavour of Stilton is added at this stage. (photo by Noriko Maegawa)

**3**. Once the rennet has been added, the milk is stirred gently with a cutting tool to ensure that the forming curds do not coagulate into massive lumps. (photo by Noriko Maegawa)

**4**. Once the rennet has done its work the milk separates out into curds and whey. The liquid whey has long been a major constituent of the pig feed that helps produce the high quality pork for Melton Mowbray's famous pies. (photo by Noriko Maegawa)

**5**. When the curds and whey have separated they are ladled by hand from the trough on to a cooling table, where the whey is drained away. (photo by Noriko Maegawa)

**6**. After the whey has been drained off, the curds are cut up into blocks. (photo by Noriko Maegawa)

**7**. The blocks of curd are transferred to a large bowl where they are crumbled by hand. Salt is then added and the mixture crumbled and turned over time after time. (photo by Noriko Maegawa)

**8**. Once mixed, the curds are placed into cylindrical moulds (or hoops) and placed on to shelving. These will be turned several times a day for the first week and then less regularly for around five weeks to ensure the even draining of the remaining whey. When the cheeses are removed from the hoops, the coats are smoothed by hand. (photo by Noriko Maegawa)

**9**. At about six weeks of age each cheese is pierced with stainless steel needles to allow air to enter the body of the cheese and activate the blue cheese mould, and so commences the magical veining process. The cheeses are then racked onto wooden boards and left to mature for several weeks. (photo by Noriko Maegawa)

**10**. Immediately before leaving the dairy each cheese is inspected for quality. Only those meeting the highest grades are released for sale as Stilton. All other cheeses are sold as 'English blue cheese'. (photo by Noriko Maegawa)

The following dairies are currently making Stilton cheese:

## Long Clawson Dairy Limited

Founded in 1911, Clawson is one of the oldest and most successful farmers' co-operatives in the UK. Based in Leicestershire's beautiful Vale of Belvoir, the company's state-of-the-art cheesemaking plants benefit from a program of on-going innovation, investment in people and technology, hygiene control, training and efficiency. All are dedicated to bringing the best quality cheeses and specialities to a discerning public.

## Cropwell Bishop Creamery

Cropwell Bishop Creamery is a small, independent family run business with origins dating back to 1847. Based on the border of Nottinghamshire and Leicestershire – two of the three counties where Stilton may be made – Cropwell Bishop Creamery has been completely modernized. Easier handling, improved hygiene and better maturing conditions have been combined with methods proven by time.

## Hartington Dairy

The Duke of Devonshire established a creamery at Hartington in the 1870s. The site was eventually bought by Thomas Nuttall, a cheesemaker from Melton Mowbray, who had already won numerous local prizes for his abilities as a maker of Stilton. The business was acquired by the Milk Marketing Board in the 1930s and the factory was extensively redeveloped on the original site in 1974. It was subsequently transferred to Dairy Crest and after a substantial redevelopment starting in 2000, was sold to Long Clawson Dairy in August 2008. The acquisition is currently being investigated by the Competition Commission.

## Tuxford & Tebbutt

Tuxford & Tebbutt Creamery, dating back to 1780, is located in Melton Mowbray, Leicestershire. The name originates from the two original owners, Mr Tuxford the Stilton man and Mr Tebbutt the pork pie man. Up until 1965, both cheese and pork pies were made on the same site. However, since 1966, Tuxford & Tebbutt has focused solely on cheesemaking. Employing over eighty staff, Tuxford & Tebbutt uses traditional cheesemaking skills and is one of only seven creameries able to produce Stilton cheese.

## Colston Bassett Dairy Limited

For over eighty-five years Colston Bassett and District Dairy has been making the finest quality Blue Stilton, 'Queen of Cheeses'. A highly skilled, dedicated and experienced team use the same time-honoured recipe and methods used by generations to make this unique, award-winning cheese, every day taking the milk from the same pastures and the same farms that founded the dairy as a co-operative in 1913.

## Quenby Hall

Blue cheese, thought to be a precursor of Blue Stilton, was produced at Quenby Hall in the eighteenth century by the then owner, Shuckburgh Ashby, and was sold in the village of Stilton. The current owner, Freddie de Lisle, restarted production of Blue Stilton in 2005 in a purpose built unit on the estate. It is already gaining a strong following.

## Websters Dairy

Saxelby. Near Melton Mowbray, Leicestershire LE14 3PH – Blue and White Stilton

## Months Earlier / Shirevale Ltd

Unit 7 Canalside Industrial Park, Kinoulton Road, Cropwell Bishop, Nottingham, NG12 3BE – White Stilton

The official mark of the Stilton Cheese Makers Association. Only cheese made according to their exacting standards is allowed to carry this badge.

# Stilton and Smoked Salmon Timbales with Horseradish

**Serves 4    Preparation time: 1 hour    Cooking Time: nil**

It is some decades since salmon were found in Leicestershire rivers, but just because they are now sourced commercially from far to the north, there is no reason not to use them. This is a deliciously light little starter that works well as a luxurious snack.

## Ingredients

3oz Stilton cheese, rind removed and crumbled
6 tablespoons red lentils
1 stalk celery, finely chopped
7oz smoked salmon
4oz light cream cheese
1 tablespoon creamed horseradish
2 tablespoons milk
12oz new potatoes
4 oz baby sweetcorn
1 bag mixed green salad
5 tablespoons rapeseed oil or vegetable oil
1 teaspoon grainy mustard
2 teaspoons lemon juice
8 chives
Black pepper

## Method

❖ Line the insides of four tea cups (or cup-sized timbale moulds) with clear plastic wrap, then line each cup up the side with smoked salmon. Set aside.

❖ To make the filling, cover the lentils with boiling water and simmer for 10 minutes until soft. Cool under running water, drain and place in a bowl with the celery, Stilton, cream cheese and horseradish.

❖ Combine these ingredients and adjust to a dropping consistency with milk. Fill the lined tea cups and refrigerate while you cook the new potatoes and warm the sweetcorn.

❖ Turn the smoked salmon timbales out onto four large plates, scatter the salad all around, then place the still warm potatoes and sweetcorn randomly through the salad.

❖ To finish, combine the oil, grainy mustard and lemon juice into a dressing and trickle over the leaves.

❖ Top each timbale with 2 chives and freshly ground black pepper to taste.

# Stilton, Bacon and Mushroom Starter

| Serves 6 | Preparation time: 15 minutes | Cooking Time: 25 minutes |

This dish is quick and easy – great for those of us who don't have all that much time to spare in the kitchen after a long day at work. The punch flavours make this a cracking dish that works equally well as a starter at dinner, a snack for lunch or a zingy main dish served with boiled potatoes and vegetables.

## Ingredients

1 tablespoon oil
1 chopped onion
1lb baby button mushrooms, halved
12 rashers streaky bacon, chopped
4oz Blue Stilton cheese, roughly chopped
8oz cream cheese
¼ pt double cream
Approx 1 oz fresh chives, snipped
3oz fresh breadcrumbs
2 teaspoons paprika
Black pepper

## Method

❖ Preheat the oven to 190°C/Gas Mark 5.

❖ Heat the oil and fry the onions, mushrooms and bacon together until browned.

❖ Share the mushroom mixture between four ramekin dishes.

❖ Beat the Stilton together with the cream cheese and cream and stir in most of the chives, reserving a few for a garnish.

❖ Season the Stilton mixture and and spoon over the top of the mushroom mixture.

❖ Toss the breadcrumbs in the paprika and sprinkle over the top of the Stilton mixture.

❖ Bake for about 25 minutes, until browned and bubbling.

❖ Serve hot with small slices of toasted French bread.


# Stilton on Horseback

| Serves 4 | Preparation time: 30 minutes | Cooking Time: 15 minutes |

This is a smashing summer dish that works as canapés to be passed around at a drinks party, or as a tasty lunch. It is best with slightly older Stilton, as the cheese acquires a smoother texture as it ages. It is, of course, a variation on the traditional classic Devils on Horseback. An advantage to this dish is that it can be prepared up to twenty-four hours in advance and then grilled at the last minute. If you are using this as a lunch dish, it should satisfy four people if served with bread and butter.

## Ingredients

6oz Stilton mature cheese, rind removed, cut into 16 pieces
2 stalks celery, thinly sliced
16 large pitted prunes, no need to soak
8oz bacon cut into thin strips about 3 inches long

## Method

❖ Make a cut down the side of each prune, put a piece of Stilton into each prune and wedge in with slices of celery.

❖ Wrap each prune in a strip of bacon and set onto a rack ready for grilling.

❖ Allow 10-12 minutes under a moderate grill, turning once.

❖ Serve warm.

# Stilton Twists

These lovely little snacks are perfect served with a glass of wine before dinner. But their real value is as a luxurious standby snack. You can make them up, then freeze them in sealed plastic bags ready to whip out and bake from frozen if unexpected guests suddenly turn up and you feel like impressing them with a magnificent home-cooked snackette and a glass of wine. These quantities should make about four dozen twists. I recommend using shop puff pastry as this is usually of good quality these days and much less effort than making it yourself. The puff pastry bought this way usually comes in two sheets per pack, but if not, cut the pastry into two equal sheets before starting.

## Ingredients

1 package puff pastry sheet
4oz Stilton Blue cheese, grated
Paprika

## Method:

❖ Thaw the puff pastry as per package instructions.
❖ Unfold the first sheet of pastry on to a cutting board and dust with paprika.
❖ Turn over and sprinkle with grated Stilton.
❖ Place second sheet pastry on top and roll lightly with a rolling pin.
❖ Dust with paprika.
❖ Cut the pastry sheet in half and the separate halves into ¼ inch wide strips.
❖ Give each strip three twists. [Freeze at this point if desired]
❖ Lightly grease a baking tray and place the twists on it, pressing ends down to anchor.
❖ In a very hot oven (225C/Gas Mark 7) for six minutes, or nine minutes if cooking from frozen.

# Blue Stilton Soup

You could enjoy this soup at any time of year, but to be honest it is best in the winter. Get a saucepan of this on the bubble before guests arrive and then wait for the compliments to start: 'Mmmmmmm something smells good', they will say. Never fails. If you have one of those handheld food liquidiser things, then use it for this recipe. Alternatively use a conventional food processor for the liquidising. Older cookbooks will advise you to press the mixture through a sieve, but that is just way too much trouble in this day and age.

## Ingredients

2oz butter
1 onion, skinned and finely chopped
2 celery sticks, cleaned and sliced
1oz flour
2fl oz dry white wine
30fl oz chicken stock
12fl oz milk
3oz Stilton cheese, crumbled
3oz English Cheddar cheese, grated
Salt and pepper
2fl oz double cream (optional)
Croutons to garnish (optional)

## Method

❖ Melt the butter in a saucepan, add the onion and celery.
❖ Fry gently for 5 minutes until soft but not browned.
❖ Stir in the flour and cook for 1 minute.
❖ Remove from heat.
❖ Stir in the wine and stock and return to heat.
❖ Bring to the boil, stirring continuously until the soup thickens, then simmer over low heat for 30 minutes.
❖ Remove the soup from the heat and allow to cool slightly.
❖ Liquidize the soup.
❖ Add the milk and heat gently.
❖ Stir in the Stilton and English Cheddar and stir while it melts.
❖ At the last minute, remove from the heat to stir in the cream, if you are using it. Do not let the soup boil after the cream has been added.
❖ Serve garnished with croutons.

# Stilton, Leek & Wild Mushroom Soup

| Serves 4 | Preparation time: 15 minutes | Cooking Time: 30 minutes |

Another soup that works best on chilly days and is guaranteed to fill your home with the most appetising of aromas. If you cannot get wild mushrooms, dried porcini mushrooms are an easily obtained alternative – simply reconstitute them as instructed on the packet before starting. If you have one of those handheld food liquidiser things, then use it for this recipe. Alternatively use a conventional food processor for the liquidising. Older cookbooks will advise you to press the mixture through a sieve, but that is just way too much trouble in this day and age.

## Ingredients

1lb leeks, white part only
2oz butter
1½ ptss vegetable stock
11fl oz milk
8oz potatoes, peeled and chopped
3oz wild mushrooms or ¾oz dried porcini mushrooms
3oz Blue Stilton cheese
4 tablespoons creamed horseradish
4 tablespoons sour cream
1 large pickled gherkin, chopped
4 sprigs of fresh chervil or parsley

## Method

❖ Split the leeks lengthways into four, wash and slice finely.
❖ Melt the butter in a large saucepan, add the leeks and soften for 3-4 minutes.
❖ Add the vegetable stock, milk, potatoes and mushrooms.
❖ Bring to the boil and simmer for 20 minutes.
❖ When the potatoes are soft, remove the soup from the heat and allow to cool slightly.
❖ Add the Stilton cheese and liquidise until smooth.
❖ Meanwhile, combine the horseradish, sour cream and gherkin in a small bowl.
❖ Serve the soup into bowls, top with a spoonful of horseradish mixture and finish with chervil or parsley to garnish.

# Roasted Spring Lamb with Stilton and Raspberry Sauce

| Serves 4 | Preparation time: 15 minutes | Cooking Time: Approx 1 hour, depending on size of lamb joint |
|---|---|---|

This dish nicely combines the different parts of Leicestershire. Stilton came from the east of the county where cows were grazed on the lush, damp grazing of the clay lowlands. The lamb comes from the west where sheep munched the rougher upland pastures. And every good country garden had a few raspberry canes in the fruit patch somewhere. Conveniently the raspberries ripened at the same time of year as the lambs got to a good size for slaughtering. These days, lamb is available year round and frozen raspberries work as well as fresh. Stuffing the joint of lamb will make it easier to carve, and will add a smashing good flavour to the meat. This recipe works equally well with shoulder of lamb, which is rather cheaper than the leg but just as succulent. Your butcher will happily bone the joint for you before you take it home.

## Ingredients

5 spring onions, chopped
2oz butter
2 teaspoons white wine vinegar
4oz fresh white breadcrumbs
2oz Blue Stilton cheese, crumbled
3 tablespoons ground hazelnuts
8oz fresh or frozen raspberries
Black pepper
A leg of lamb, boned
Gravy
4 tablespoons red wine
11fl oz chicken stock
2 teaspoons cornflour
1 teaspoon Dijon mustard

## Method

❖ Cook the spring onions lightly in the butter to soften, add the vinegar and set aside.

❖ Stir the breadcrumbs into the onion mixture

❖ Add the Stilton, hazelnuts, half the raspberries and seasoning.

❖ Preheat the oven to 200°C/Gas Mark 6.

❖ Open the joint of lamb flat and season well.

❖ Spoon in the stuffing, then roll up the meat and tie with string.

❖ Place the lamb in a roasting pan and cook, allowing 15 minutes per pound, boned weight.

❖ When the lamb is cooked, transfer to a warm plate, cover and allow to rest.

❖ Meanwhile, simmer the wine, chicken stock and mustard in a saucepan.

❖ Add the juices from the roasting tin and bring to the boil.

❖ Combine the cornflour with 2 teaspoons of cold water and add to the gravy to thicken.

❖ At the last moment, add the remaining raspberries.

❖ Place the lamb on a carving dish, the gravy in a large jug and serve.

# Stilton and Roasted Turkey Wraps

| Serves 4 | Preparation time: 20 minutes | Cooking Time: nil |

This dish comes from America where it has been used to market Stilton cheese alongside the traditional American festival of Thanksgiving, when they roast a turkey. In this country it is better suited to the aftermath of Christmas when most families have a good deal of cold turkey knocking about the house. The quantities given here are for four wraps, but you can simply increase or decrease the quantities depending on how many hungry mouths you have to feed. This is one of those dishes that is best eaten with the hands – good and messy, the children will love it.

## Ingredients

6oz crumbled Stilton cheese
4 tablespoons mayonnaise
A large pinch of ground ginger
1 ripe pear, peeled and mashed
4 flour tortillas, 9 inch diameter size
1 ripe pear, unpeeled, thinly sliced
12oz cooked turkey, thinly sliced
12oz fresh spinach leaves
Salt and pepper

## Method:

❖ In a bowl, mash 4oz of the Stilton with the mayonnaise, ginger and mashed pear jam.

❖ Spread this on one side of the tortillas.

❖ Down the centre of each tortilla lay a row of unpeeled, sliced pear.

❖ Top the pear with the turkey, then spinach leaves.

❖ Sprinkle with salt and pepper to taste.

❖ Sprinkle with the remaining crumbled Stilton.

❖ Roll up securely.

❖ Serve.

# Stilton Tagliatelle

| Serves 4 | Preparation time: 5 minutes | Cooking Time: 8 minutes |

Elegant, but quick and easy to prepare, this makes a superb supper dish for those of us who are short of time after work, but also makes for a cracking centrepiece for an impromptu meal at home if friends come to call.

## Ingredients

10oz tagliatelle pasta
4oz crumbled Stilton cheese
250ml sour cream or fromage frais
1 egg lightly beaten
Pepper
1 tablespoon fresh flat leaf parsley, chopped

## Method

❖ Cook tagliatelle in boiling, salted water following package directions; drain thoroughly.

❖ Toss cooked pasta with the Stilton, sour cream, beaten egg and pepper and mix well over a low heat until the egg is cooked through and the Stilton has melted into the pasta.

❖ Serve immediately, garnished with parsley.

# Stilton Risotto with Winter Squash, Sage & Walnuts

| Serves 4 | Preparation time: 10 minutes | Cooking Time: Approx 30 minutes |
|---|---|---|

This dish is surprisingly easy to make given the sophisticated end product. It is great as a warming family supper in mid-winter, and is always a hit with friends. If you cannot get hold of fresh sage, you can use dried sage.

## Ingredients

1 tablespoons vegetable oil
2oz walnuts, roughly chopped
½oz butter
1 onion, chopped
1 tablespoon freshly chopped sage
12oz arborio risotto rice
2 pts vegetable stock, boiling
11oz winter squash, deseeded, peeled and roughly chopped
3oz Blue Stilton cheese
4 sprigs fresh sage for garnish (optional)

## Method

❖ Heat the vegetable oil in a large saucepan, add half of the chopped walnuts and allow to brown.
❖ Spoon the nuts onto a plate and set aside.
❖ Add the butter, onions and chopped sage to the pan and soften for about 6 minutes.
❖ Stir in the rice to absorb the cooking juices.
❖ Add the stock and the chopped squash, then simmer, uncovered, for 15 minutes.
❖ Switch off the heat, crumble in the Stilton, add the remaining chopped walnuts, cover and allow to finish cooking in its own heat for 5 minutes.
❖ If you have it, serve each portion garnished with a sprig of fresh sage.

# Fish with Stilton and Mediterranean Vegetable Topping

| Serves 4 | Preparation time: 15 minutes | Cooking Time: 15 minutes |
|---|---|---|

## Ingredients

4 x 5 oz thick cod or haddock fillets
1 tablespoon olive oil
1 red onion, peeled and sliced
1 red pepper, deseeded and sliced
1 teaspoon balsamic vinegar
1 knob of butter
5oz Blue Stilton cheese, crumbled
1 handful of basil leaves, torn
Salt and pepper

## Method

❖ Preheat the oven to 200°C/Gas Mark 6.
❖ Heat the oil in a heavy based frying pan, add the onion and pepper and cook for 5 minutes until soft.
❖ Add the balsamic vinegar and continue to cook for a further 5 minutes until the vegetables are soft and starting to brown.
❖ Meanwhile, lightly butter four foil squares measuring about 8 inches.
❖ Place each piece of fish in the middle of a square.
❖ Top with the onion and pepper mix.
❖ Pile the Stilton on top of the vegetables and sprinkle with half the basil.
❖ Fold the foil into a parcel and bake for 15 minutes.
❖ Serve with an extra sprinkle of basil, sea salt and pepper.

# Stilton Meatballs

**Serves 4**     **Preparation time: 10 minutes**     **Cooking Time: 20 minutes**

Meatballs are a wonderfully versatile dish. They go beautifully with noodles, as here, or with pasta, mashed potatoes or rice. Leftovers can be taken on picnics or used in a packed lunch the next day. The addition of the Stilton gives an innovative twist to this dish. This recipe is for lamb mince, but beef mince can be used if preferred.

## Ingredients

1 onion, finely chopped
1 clove garlic, finely chopped
5oz white breadcrumbs
1lb lamb mince
4oz extra mature Blue Stilton cheese, crumbled
1 egg
1 bunch fresh parsley, chopped
2 tablespoons oil
1 onion sliced
6oz mushrooms, sliced
14oz can of chopped tomatoes
2 tablespoons tomato puree
150ml/5 fl oz lamb stock
(for a vegetarian alternative replace with vegetable stock)
Salt and pepper
10oz noodles

## Method

❖ Preheat the oven to 200°C/Gas Mark 6.

❖ Place the chopped onion, garlic and breadcrumbs in a bowl and mix in the mince and extra mature Stilton.

❖ Stir in the egg, parsley and seasonings.

❖ Shape the mixture into small walnut sized balls, with damp hands, and arrange in a roasting tin.

❖ Bake for 20 minutes, or until browned.

❖ Lift out of the pan with a slotted spoon discarding any fat.

❖ Meanwhile, heat the oil and fry the sliced onion until starting to brown.

❖ Add the mushrooms and continue to fry for 2 minutes before adding the tomatoes, tomato puree and lamb stock.

❖ Bring the mixture to the boil and simmer for 10 minutes, until it starts to thicken.

❖ Add the meatballs to the sauce and cook gently for 4 minutes, until hot.

❖ Meanwhile, cook the noodles as per the packet instructions.

❖ Pour the meatball mixture over the noodles and serve.

# Stilton Soda Bread

**Serves 4**　　　　　**Preparation time: 10 minutes**　　　　**Cooking Time: 35 minutes**

Soda bread is a traditional way of making a tasty bread without all the messing about with bread yeast that some cooks think to be a bit too much trouble. Adding a little Stilton makes the soda bread even more irresistible! Delicious served warm from the oven, torn into hunks.

## Ingredients

11oz wholemeal flour
11oz plain white flour
1 teaspoon bicarbonate of soda
5oz Blue Stilton, cubed
1oz Blue Stilton, crumbled finely
1pt skimmed milk

## Method

❖ Sift the flours into a mixing bowl with the bicarbonate of soda.

❖ Stir in the cubed Stilton and enough milk to make the dough soft.

❖ Turn out the dough on to a floured board and knead lightly.

❖ Shape into a round loaf and score a cross into the top.

❖ Place the loaf on a lightly greased baking sheet.

❖ Cook in a preheated fairly hot oven (220°C/Gas Mark 7) for 35 minutes until just brown.

❖ Remove from the oven, sprinkle over the crumbled Stilton and return to the oven for 1 minute to melt the cheese.


# Stilton Mashed Potato with Toasted Walnuts

**Serves 4**　　　　**Preparation time: 5 minutes**　　　　**Cooking Time: Approx 20 minutes**

Mashed potatoes are especially good combined with creamy Stilton cheese and toasted walnuts. This Stilton mash is great served with sausages and onion gravy to give a novel twist to that old favourite of Bangers and Mash. It is also a perfect accompaniment to any roast joint of meat. It could even be served as a lunch dish on its own. I'm told that nutmeg makes this dish even more special, but I don't care for it myself so I have made it an optional ingredient.

## Ingredients

4oz Stilton cheese, rind removed and crumbled
2lbs (about 4 large) potatoes
2oz walnuts, roughly chopped
6fl oz milk
Salt and pepper
Nutmeg (optional)

## Method

❖ Peel and quarter the potatoes, cover with cold water, bring to a boil and cook for 20-25 minutes until they begin to fall apart.

❖ Drain the potatoes, leaving a little of the cooking water in the pan.

❖ Mash the potatoes until there are no lumps.

❖ Stir in the milk, walnuts, Stilton and season to taste with salt, pepper and (if liked) nutmeg.

❖ Adjust the consistency of the mashed potatoes with milk until it begins to fall from the spoon.

# Stilton Party Cheesecake

Serves 6      Preparation time: 20 minutes      Cooking Time: 3 hours

This cheesecake makes a grand finale to any meal. The delicate aroma and taste that are uniquely Stilton come through beautifully. An added advantage to this dish is that it can be frozen and kept until needed.

## Ingredients

8oz Blue Stilton
16oz cream cheese
3 eggs
4oz sugar
1oz flour
8fl oz sour cream
2 tablespoons dry vermouth or lemon juice
1 teaspoon vanilla essence
1oz butter or margarine, melted
6oz crushed gingernut biscuits

## Method

❖ Preheat oven to 160°C/Gas Mark 3
❖ Place crumbled Stilton, sugar and cream cheese into a bowl and beat with an electric mixer until well blended.
❖ Beat in eggs, one at a time until smooth and creamy.
❖ Add vanilla and stir in flour, sour cream and dry vermouth or lemon juice until well blended.
❖ Meanwhile, combine the melted butter and crushed biscuits in a bowl until well mixed.
❖ Press the biscuit mixture into the bottom of a 9 inch loose-bottomed flan dish.
❖ Pour cheese mixture over the biscuit base.
❖ Bake in the oven for about 1 hour, or until firm.
❖ Turn off heat and let cake cool in oven for 1 hour.
❖ Cover dish with cling film and refrigerate until ready to serve.

# Burgundy Pears with Stilton Cream

Serves 4      Preparation time: 15 minutes      Cooking Time: 15 minutes

This dessert dish is easy to prepare, but will make any cook look like a world-class chef. I'd rustle this up as a dessert at a dinner after a robust main course involving beef or game.

## Ingredients

4 ripe pears
½ bottle of good red wine
2oz sugar
1 bayleaf
Piece of lemon peel
Piece of orange peel
½ cinnamon stick (or ½ teaspoon cinnamon powder)
6 black peppercorns
2 cloves
4oz Stilton
6fl oz cider
5fl oz double cream

## Method

❖ Peel the pears, removing the core but leaving the stalks in.
❖ Place in a large pan with the wine, sugar, bayleaf, lemon peel, orange peel, cinnamon, black peppercorns and cloves.
❖ Gently bring to a boil.
❖ Skim off any impurities and simmer for 8 minutes until the pears are just cooked and allow to cool.
❖ Meanwhile, combine the cheese, cider and cream in a pan.
❖ Simmer for 2 minutes, then liquidize.
❖ Place each pear in a dish.
❖ Pour a little of the cream over each pear and serve the remainder in a sauceboat.

# White Stilton Rice Pudding with Raspberry Coulis

| Serves 4 | Preparation time: 20 minutes | Cooking Time: 2 hours |

Many of us remember rice pudding from school dinners and have not eaten it since. No wonder, rice pudding can all too easily become a gelatinous mess, but this version is light and tasty while the Stilton adds a rich and creamy bite to this traditional recipe.

## Ingredients

1 pt milk
1oz caster sugar
6oz White Stilton cheese
finely chopped
1½oz pudding rice
8oz fresh raspberries
8 lemon balm leaves
3 tablespoons icing sugar

## Method

❖ Preheat the oven to 150°C/Gas Mark 2.

❖ Gently heat the milk and sugar in a saucepan until the sugar has dissolved.

❖ Add the White Stilton and pudding rice and warm gently for approximately 2 minutes – do not boil.

❖ Transfer the mixture to a 17.5cm (7in) square ovenproof dish and cook for one hour, stirring gently every 15 minutes to break up any skin forming.

❖ After an hour, stop stirring and cook for a further hour until thick.

❖ Remove from the oven and allow to cool slightly.

❖ Meanwhile, blend half the raspberries and the icing sugar together until smooth then press the through a sieve to remove the pips and form the coulis.

❖ Using an 8cm round cutter, stamp out four circles from the rice pudding mixture – this step may be omitted if liked.

❖ Place each portion on a dessert plate. Spoon the raspberry coulis around the edge and decorate with the remaining raspberries and lemon balm leaves.

# Apple and White Stilton Tarts

| Serves 4 | Preparation time: 60 minutes | Cooking Time: 25 minutes |

You don't get much better as a sophisticated dessert than this dish. The richness of Stilton complimented by the sharpness of the fruit creates an elegant dessert that is a classic combination of cheese and apple.

## Ingredients

1 pack ready-made dessert shortcrust pastry.
16oz cooking apples, peeled, cored and sliced
3oz white sugar
4oz White Stilton cheese finely chopped
¼ pt double cream
3 eating apples cored and quartered, but not peeled
2 tablespoons lemon juice
3 tablespoons apricot jam

## Method

❖ Preheat the oven to 190°C/Gas Mark 6.

❖ Divide the dough into four equal pieces and roll out each one until large enough to line a 4 inch fluted flan tin.

❖ Place pastry in flan tins and chill for 30 minutes before baking for 15-20 minutes until golden brown, then set aside to cool.

❖ Meanwhile, place the cooking apples in a pan together with the remaining sugar and one tablespoon water.

❖ Heat gently, then simmer until it forms a puree-like consistency.

❖ Stir in the White Stilton and leave to cool slightly.

❖ Share the apple and Stilton puree between the four pastry cases and level out.

❖ Thinly slice the eating apples and toss in lemon juice.

❖ Arrange the apple slices in a neat, overlapping pattern on top of the Stilton and apple puree.

❖ Gently heat the apricot jam in a pan with 1 tablespoon of water until melted, then spoon over the fruit.

❖ Put the tarts under a hot grill for 3-4 minutes, until lightly browned.

❖ Serve warm with cream or custard.

I am deeply indebted to the Stilton Cheesemakers Association for their help with this chapter. I would recommend any reader who wants to learn more about this magnificent cheese, how it is produced and what you can do with it to visit their website at www.stiltoncheese.com. I must also thank Tuxford & Tebbutt.

In 1889 the famous book *Three Men in a Boat* was written by Jerome K. Jerome. The book was about three men who go on a boating holiday up the Thames. As they are preparing to set off, the three men discuss what foods they should take with them. One of the men, Harris, suggests taking a whole cheese that they can carve at as they row. Another, George, objects. The narrator then tells of the time that he had an unpleasant encounter with some cheeses. He does not name the cheeses, but if they were Stilton's they must have been well past their best. The book continues:

> I remember a friend of mine, buying a couple of cheeses at Liverpool. Splendid cheeses they were, ripe and mellow, and with a two hundred horse-power scent about them that might have been warranted to carry three miles, and knock a man over at two hundred yards. I was in Liverpool at the time, and my friend said that if I didn't mind he would get me to take them

back with me to London, as he should not be coming up for a day or two himself, and he did not think the cheeses ought to be kept much longer.

'Oh, with pleasure, dear boy,' I replied, 'with pleasure.'

I called for the cheeses, and took them away in a cab. It was a ramshackle affair, dragged along by a knock-kneed, broken-winded somnambulist, which his owner, in a moment of enthusiasm, during conversation, referred to as a horse. I put the cheeses on the top, and we started off at a shamble that would have done credit to the swiftest steam-roller ever built, and all went merry as a funeral bell, until we turned the corner. There, the wind carried a whiff from the cheeses full on to our steed. It woke him up, and, with a snort of terror, he dashed off at three miles an hour. The wind still blew in his direction, and before we reached the end of the street he was laying himself out at the rate of nearly four miles an hour, leaving the cripples and stout old ladies simply nowhere.

It took two porters as well as the driver to hold him in at the station; and I do not think they would have done it, even then, had not one of the men had the presence of mind to put a handkerchief over his nose, and to light a bit of brown paper.

I took my ticket, and marched proudly up the platform, with my cheeses, the people falling back respectfully on either side. The train was crowded, and I had to get into a carriage where there were already seven other people. One crusty old gentleman objected, but I got in, notwithstanding; and, putting my cheeses upon the rack, squeezed down with a pleasant smile, and said it was a warm day.

A few moments passed, and then the old gentleman began to fidget.

'Very close in here,' he said.

'Quite oppressive,' said the man next him.

And then they both began sniffing, and, at the third sniff, they caught it right on the chest, and rose up without another word and went out. And then a stout lady got up, and said it was disgraceful that a respectable married woman should be harried about in this way, and gathered up a bag and eight parcels and went. The remaining four passengers sat on for a while, until a solemn-looking man in the corner, who, from his dress and general appearance, seemed to belong to the undertaker class, said it put him in mind of dead baby; and the other three passengers tried to get out of the door at the same time, and hurt themselves.

I smiled at the black gentleman, and said I thought we were going to have the carriage to ourselves; and he laughed pleasantly, and said that some people made such a fuss over a little thing. But even he grew strangely depressed after we had started, and so, when we reached Crewe, I asked him to come and have a drink. He accepted, and we forced our way into the buffet, where we yelled, and stamped, and waved our umbrellas for a quarter of an hour; and then a young lady came, and asked us if we wanted anything.

'What's yours?' I said, turning to my friend.

'I'll have half-a-crown's worth of brandy, neat, if you please, miss,' he responded.

And he went off quietly after he had drunk it and got into another carriage, which I thought mean.

From Crewe I had the compartment to myself, though the train was crowded. As we drew up at the different stations, the people, seeing my empty carriage, would rush for it. 'Here y' are, Maria; come along, plenty of room.' 'All right, Tom; we'll get in here,' they would shout. And they would run along, carrying heavy bags, and fight round the door to get in first. And one would open the door and mount the steps, and stagger back into the arms of the man behind him; and they would all come and have a sniff, and then droop off and squeeze into other carriages, or pay the difference and go first.

# Seven

# FROM THE OVEN

Baking food in the oven generally involves one of four basic methods: bread, biscuits, pastry or cake. The cooks of Leicestershire have long been at the forefront of all four sorts of oven cooking, and have produced a wide range of tasty treats to tempt the palate.

The oldest of the four basic types of oven cooking was in fact developed before ovens were in widespread use. Bread was at first baked by forming it into round, flat discs and slapping it down on stones heated to high temperatures by being placed in front of a really hot fire. By the time ovens were in widespread use across the area, around 700 BC or thereabouts, their main purpose was the baking of bread.

Bread remained a key part of the diet of most people throughout Roman times. It fell rather out of favour in the early centuries of English times, but by 1100 was once again rising in favour

A selection of English breads as depicted in 1860 with a windmill in the background.

King John introduced laws concerning the baking and sale of bread that were to outlive him by some 600 years.

and importance. In about 1208, King John introduced a new law that he called the Assize of Bread. John instructed that this law was to be read out in every market place in England and had to be enforced by the local magistrates. It was read out in Leicester, and other towns in the county, and it seems to have been rigorously enforced. King John has been much maligned by history, but with his Assize of Bread he scored a real success. It remained in force, updated form time to time, until 1815.

King John's law laid down a host of rules and regulations about the baking of bread and its sale. The key problem was that bread rises when it is baked, so it is next to impossible for a customer to tell just by looking at the bread loaf how much bread it contained. An associated problem concerned the quality of the flour used to make the loaf. Unscrupulous bakers were known to mix all sorts of cheaper powders into the flour before the dough was made to reduce their costs. Notoriously, powdered chalk was added to flour to make a poor quality flour look whiter and to increase the weight of the finished loaf.

Some of the provisions of the Assize of Bread were technical matters that could be enforced only by the magistrates visiting a bakery to test the quality of flour, dough and other materials. But some clauses were easy for everybody to understand and any customer who thought he was being cheated could go straight to the local magistrate, loaf in hand, to register his complaint.

Under the Assize of Bread, all loaves had to cost exactly the same. This was a farthing in King John's day, but it had risen to a penny by the reign of King George III when the law was abolished. To take account of the different prices for different grades of flour, bakers were instructed to bake their loaves in different sizes. For instance a basic wholemeal loaf was to weigh twice as much as a loaf of white bread. The magistrates were expected to lay down the actual weight of the standard farthing loaf of wholemeal bread – called the omniblado – from time to time to reflect the changing price of wheat. A loaf one year might be heavier than one baked the year before. Whenever they changed the weight of the standard loaf in their town, magistrates had to have the change announced in the market place.

Penalties for bakers who broke the law were severe and swift. If a baker produced a loaf of the wrong weight he was to be dragged through the streets of the town tied to a wooden hurdle pulled by a horse with the offending loaf of bread around his neck. If the same baker was convicted a second time, he was again dragged through the streets, but instead of then being released had to spend twenty-four hours in the stocks. For a third offence, the dishonest baker was dragged through the streets, put in the stocks and then his oven was smashed to pieces by the magistrates, after which he was thrown out of the town.

The Square, Market Harborough.

The market place in Market Harborough as it appeared in 1910. It was here that a novel recipe for using up leftover bread sauce was produced.

With such severe penalties to be had, it is no wonder that bakers went out of their way to ensure that they obeyed the law. It was this that led to the custom of a 'baker's dozen' being composed of thirteen items, not twelve. A bread roll had to weigh one twelfth as much as a loaf, and penalties for having undersized rolls were almost as bad as for selling undersized loafs. If a customer asked for a dozen rolls, therefore, he was usually given thirteen to make absolutely certain that the dozen rolls weighed as much as or more than a loaf.

Biscuits were probably developed at about the same time in the prehistoric past as bread, though there is less evidence for them being made. Not all biscuits were baked, as one Roman recipe from AD 100 shows:

Take some wheat flour and simmer in hot milk so that it forms a stiff paste. Spread it on a plate. When cold, cut up the paste into pieces and fry them in oil. Take out and pour honey over them.

In Britain, though, most biscuits seem to have been baked. By medieval times, spiced biscuits were hugely popular – gingerbread was first mentioned in 1265. By 1400 most of the modern types of biscuit had been developed and most were being baked in Leicestershire. Since then the development of the biscuit has been more a matter of changing tastes and fashions than of technique or basic ingredients.

Also finding its way into ovens during Roman times was pastry. This early pastry was very similar to what we now call shortcrust pastry, being made of flour and fat rubbed together, then mixed into a paste with water. The Romans did not do very much with pastry. The cookbooks

Despite the end of large scale grain farming in the county at the end of the nineteenth century, a few craft mills have survived. This flour is from Whissendun Mill.

of the time treat it very much as we use aluminium foil today. It is recommended for encasing joints of meat, fish or other items that the cook wants to cook in an oven while trapping the natural juices that would otherwise run out.

It was not until the English came to Leicestershire that anything more imaginative was done with pastry. Once the English were baking in ovens in Leicestershire, however, things really began to take off. It was not long before there was a whole range of pies, spiced pastries and other delicacies bulging from the cookbooks that circulated among town bakers and the cooks employed by noblemen and gentry. In the thirteenth century these tended to be very heavy dishes by modern standards, but by the fifteenth century were becoming lighter delicacies.

The fourth type of baked good, cake, made a surprisingly late entry into Leicestershire ovens. The word cake was in use from at least AD 850 and probably much earlier. At that date the word did not refer to the cake as we know it today, but to what we would call buns. These were breads that used yeast as a raising agent but which were made with extra, rich ingredients such as butter, sugar, fruits and spices. This type of cake remained the only type on offer for over a thousand years until the Tudor period.

The practice of making special cakes for celebratory events was begun around 1400. Wedding cakes, birthday cakes, funeral cakes, Christmas cakes, Easter cakes and a host of others found their way into bakers' shops. They were invariably large and lavishly decorated. One recipe from 1450 for a 'special day cake' involved the baker using 7lb flour, 4lb currants, 2lb butter, 1pt cream, twelve eggs, 2lb sugar and 'spyces to taste'. The smaller hot cross bun as a special cake for Easter was invented around 1620.

Around 1550, or perhaps a little earlier, bakers began to make a 'cake' that used beaten eggs as the raising agent. This was the ancestor of our modern sponge cake, which contains no fat but does have a high proportion of eggs. The egg whites are beaten until they are stiff, then gently folded into the rest of the ingredients. This ensures that the thousands of tiny air bubbles trapped in the whipped egg whites remain within the cake mix. When the cake goes into the oven, the heat expands the air bubbles, causing the cake to rise. The technique can be used successfully only for small cakes. Any cake requiring more than half a pound of flour continued to be raised with yeast.

The art of cake baking might have progressed no further than this were it not for the fact that a lady living in Birmingham realised that she was allergic to yeast. Elizabeth Bird was married to a chemist by the name of Alfred Bird, who enjoyed nothing better after his shop was closed than

The grand nineteenth-century Corn Market in Melton Mowbray. The nineteenth century was a time of economic hardship for cereal farmers and the establishment of market buildings such as this was an attempt to boost flagging sales and profit margins. The efforts failed and cereal farming in Leicestershire had collapsed by 1885.

tinkering about with chemicals to see what he could produce. His wife's allergy interested him in the problem of how to make bread rise without using yeast.

Bird soon realised that the key was to develop a powder that was inert when dry and which could be mixed easily with flour. However, that powder then had to produce gas when it was mixed with water. The effect of this in cooking was that when the powder was thoroughly mixed in with the flour and then with water to form a dough, it would release millions of tiny gas bubbles which would expand hugely when baked at a high temperature and so raise the bread. Bird settled down to months of experiments to find the best chemicals for the purpose. He eventually settled on a blend of tartaric acid and bicarbonate of soda which he dubbed 'baking powder', by which name it is still sold today.

By way of an encore, Bird went on to invent the custard powder which bear's his name and which made him a fortune.

The new baking powder was never very popular with bread bakers, though the resulting soda bread is a delicious treat in its own right. Where it did prove hugely popular was with housewives who wanted to bake a small, dainty cake for their family. By the time Mrs Beeton published her seminal work in 1861, baking powder was on the pantry shelf of nearly every home in Britain. She specified it for use in some 90 per cent of her cake recipes. For a long time baking powder was sold as a separate ingredient, but these days it is more usually found already mixed in with flour in the form of self-raising flour.

By 1870 the various techniques and ingredients needed to produce bread, biscuits, pastries and cakes were in place. The bakers and housewives of Leicestershire set to with a will and soon developed a uniquely tasty and satisfying range of recipes.

# Hunting Cake

**Preparation time: 15 minutes          Cooking time: 2 hours 10 minutes**

This astonishing rich cake was developed in the mid-nineteenth century. It was traditionally served to huntsmen as they came in from the fox hunt, and was the first sustenance to be pushed into their hands after a long day's riding.

## Ingredients

4oz butter
4oz sugar
4 eggs
8oz self-raising flour
4oz ground almonds
8oz mixed sultanas and currants
2oz glacé cherries
2oz flaked almonds
½pt sherry

## Method

❖ Preheat the oven to 160°C/Gas Mark 3.
❖ Cream together the butter and sugar until fluffy and white.
❖ Separate the eggs, beating the yolks and whites separately.
❖ Add the egg yolks gradually to the butter-sugar mixture.
❖ Mix the flour with the fruits and almonds and add gradually to the butter-sugar-egg mixture.
❖ Stir in half the sherry.
❖ Carefully fold in the egg whites which have been beaten until they are stiff.
❖ Pour the mixture into a well-greased and lined 8 inch cake tin.
❖ Bake for 2 hours or until done.
❖ Remove from the oven and pour the rest of the sherry over the cake.
❖ Leave to cool before removing from the cake tin.

# Harby Cake

**Serves: 12          Preparation time: 10 minutes          Cooking time: 2 hours**

This recipe came from a legendary cook who lived in the village of Harby during Queen Victoria's reign and was widely known as 'Aunt Lucy'. I don't know her real name, but if this recipe is anything to go by she deserves her fame.

## Ingredients

8oz butter
8oz sugar
1lb self raising flour
8oz currants
2oz flaked almonds
8oz prunes, stoned
4oz mixed candied peel
A little grated nutmeg
5 eggs

## Method

❖ Preheat the oven to 180°C/Gas Mark 4.
❖ Cream the butter and sugar together until fluffy.
❖ Add the dry ingredients and mix.
❖ Beat the eggs and add a bit at a time to the mixture.
❖ If necessary add a little milk until the mixture is of a soft consistency.
❖ Place in a well greased cake tin and bake for 2 hours or until done.

# Whetstone Cakes

This recipe was first recorded in 1741 and has been a traditional favourite in Leicestershire ever since. This rich version is the oldest that I could find. A more recent version produces a lighter final cake using 12oz flour and 4oz each of sugar and butter and 2 eggs, but is otherwise very similar.

## Ingredients

10oz flour
10oz butter
10oz caster sugar
1 teaspoon carraway seeds
3 eggs
Rosewater

## Method

❖ Beat together the butter and sugar until white and fluffy.
❖ Add the carraway seeds and mix well.
❖ Beat together the eggs, then add them gradually to the mixture.
❖ Add in the flour, mixing gently.
❖ Add just enough rose water to produce a soft dough.
❖ Knead the dough until smooth, then roll out so that it is as thin as a wafer.
❖ Cut out circles of dough about 2 inches in diameter.
❖ Place the dough circles on to a greased baking tray.
❖ Bake in a cool oven (160°C/Gas Mark 3) for 20 minutes.

King Henry VII is presented with the crown of England after winning the Battle of Bosworth in Leicestershire. If local legend is to be believed, he was also presented with a plate of cakes that had been baked for his rival, Richard III. The cakes are now known as Bosworth Jumbles.

# Bosworth Jumbles

According to the version of the story I was told, these tasty little cakes gained their name from the Battle of Bosworth, fought on 22 August 1485. This was the last major battle of the War of the Roses which saw Yorkist King Richard III defeated by the Lancastrian Henry, who went on to found the Tudor dynasty as King Henry VII. Richard had gathered his army in Leicester, heading west as soon as his scouts brought in definite news of the enemy's position. Richard camped on Albion Hill on the night of 21 August. Next morning his cook baked Richard these tasty little cakes to carry with him in a pouch so that he could whip them out for a quick snack in a break from the fighting. In the event, Richard rode out to battle before they were ready and was killed in the battle. The cakes were, therefore, scoffed up by the victorious Henry Tudor that evening. Personally I think that the original cakes must have been round, not 's' shaped. A thin, curly shape is not a robust one to carry around in a pouch all day. In any case, the 's' was a symbol of the Lancastrian cause – Henry himself wore a gold necklace of interlinked 's' shaped links. I suspect the shaping of the cakes into 's' came after the battle as a tribute to the winner. Whatever the truth of their origin, they are very tasty little snacks – which is all that really matters.

## Ingredients

6oz butter
6oz caster sugar
1 egg
Grated rind of 1 lemon
8oz flour

## Method

❖ Preheat the oven to 180°C/Gas Mark 4.

❖ Beat together the butter and sugar until it is white and fluffy.

❖ Beat the egg well, then gradually add to the butter-sugar mix.

❖ Add the grated lemon rid and stir well.

❖ Add the flour a little at a time to form a stiff mixture.

❖ Divide the mixture into small pieces and form into an 'S' shape.

❖ Place on a greased baking tray

❖ Bake for 20 minutes or until golden brown.

# Belvoir Buns

It was the 7th Duke of Rutland who made these buns so popular. He loved them himself, and had them served to all his guests at Belvoir Castle overlooking the beautiful Vale of Belvoir – hence their name. They are first recorded as being served in 1869. Most people do not these days have access to fresh yeast, but dried yeast works just as well. Be careful to follow the instructions carefully to make up a mix equivalent to ½oz of fresh yeast. If you have a bread machine, you can save yourself a lot of time and effort by using it set to the bun programme, but remove the dough at the end of the 'rise' stage to be rolled out and baked as described below.

## Ingredients

¼ pt milk
½oz fresh yeast (or dried equivalent prepared as per packet instructions)
4oz sugar
1lb flour
Salt
2oz butter
4oz mixed dried fruit, chopped
Milk

## Method

❖ Add the yeast to the milk, add 1teaspoon sugar and stir until dissolved.

❖ Place the milk mixture in a warm place until frothy – usually about 15 minutes.

❖ Meanwhile, rub the butter into the flour.

❖ Stir the sugar and a pinch of salt into the flour-butter mix.

❖ Add the milk-yeast mixture and stir in well.

❖ Add half the dried fruit, working in with the fingers.

❖ Turn the dough on to a floured surface and knead until smooth – usually about 10 minutes.

❖ Leave in a warm place until doubled in size.

❖ Knead the dough again for 5 minutes.

❖ Roll out the dough to be about ½ inch thick.

❖ Sprinkle the remaining dried fruit over the dough, then roll it up.

❖ Cut the roll into pieces about 1 inch wide.

❖ Place the pieces on a greased baking tray, flat side down.

❖ Leave in a warm place for 30 minutes to rise.

❖ Brush with milk to glaze if liked.

❖ Bake in a fairly hot oven (220°C/Gas Mark 7) for 10 minutes.

# Crispy Biscuits

**Preparation time: 15 minutes**　　**Cooking time: 14 minutes**

These plain biscuits come out very snappy and brittle. They are a great snack when served with something savoury such as cheese or pâté.

## Ingredients

1lb flour
1 egg
Milk

## Method

❖ Separate the egg yolk from the white.

❖ Add the egg yolk and a little milk to the flour.

❖ Continue to add milk until the mixture forms a stiff paste.

❖ Roll out the paste very thinly on a floured board.

❖ Cut into rounds about 2 inches across.

❖ Place on a greased baking sheet.

❖ Bake in a fairly cool oven (160°C/Gas Mark 3) until golden brown, about 14 minutes.

# Market Harborough Savoury

Serves 4 (if using 1pt bread sauce)    Preparation time: 5 minute    Cooking time: 25 minutes

Bread sauce was originally a way to use up stale leftover bread. This recipe is a way to use up stale leftover bread sauce! I don't really know its name but it comes from a lady from Market Harborough, so that is the name I have used.

## Ingredients

Leftover bread sauce
Milk
Grated cheese – whatever is to hand will do
Butter

## Method

❖ If the bread sauce is more than a couple of days old, stir in some fresh milk to loosen the texture.

❖ Butter a baking dish and pour in the bread sauce.

❖ Scatter over the top of the sauce the grated cheese.

❖ Bake in a cool oven (160°C/Gas Mark 3) until the top browns over, about 25 minutes.

# Eight

# FRUIT AND VEGETABLES

The phrase 'Beanbelly Leicestershire' is not one that you hear very often these days, but only a generation or two back the county was famous for its production and consumption of beans. I have seen another phrase recorded that gives the same message: 'Shake a Leicestershire yeoman by te collar and you will hear the beans rattle in his belly'. It is a surprise, therefore, that recipes collected in the county tend not to involve beans very much. Perhaps they were considered to be a poor man's food and so did not tend to get recorded.

Beans, and other varieties of fruit and vegetable, have traditionally been produced in the working sections of the large country gardens that were usual across rural Leicestershire. These lovely products did not often get far beyond the household that produced them, for neither fruit nor vegetables were popular as a commercial crop in the county. The fruits and vegetables that did make it into towns were usually either surplus country produce or came from commercial market gardens further afield, usually to the south.

For centuries, a key problem with fruit and vegetables was that they tended to go off rather quickly. Most were eaten when they were in season and were completely unavailable for the rest of the year. A lot of effort went into finding crops that would produce edible foods outside of the usual growing season. The advent of the Brussels sprout which could be harvested from November through to February was a real boon for the winter. They first came to Leicestershire in about 1690, almost certainly brought over from their native land by soldiers and others who came to England with William of Orange, husband of Queen Mary II, who arrived in 1688. The cultivation of this useful winter green spread rapidly and by 1720 was an established feature of the Christmas feast, as it has remained ever since.

Other varieties have originated in the county itself. The Annie Elizabeth is a cooking apple that originated in Knighton, Leicestershire in 1857. The apple is round, heavy and has a golden yellow colour when ripe. It stores well and cooks beautifully. The blossom is bright pink and profusive, so this is a popular variety to be grown where it can be seen and enjoyed.

Another Leicestershire apple is the Dumelow's Seedling, sometimes called the Wellington, which originated in Ashby de la Zouch in the 1790s. This is another cooker with highly ornamental blossom. It gives a heavy crop of green apples, streaked with broken red lines when ripe. It tolerates cold weather well and the blossom can survive light frosts. It was traditionally used for commercially produced mincemeat and is rarely sold retail.

In 1935 these two cookers were crossed to produce the Belvoir Seedling, another successful cooker that is grown extensively on the Belvoir Estate. Grown alongside it is the Barnack Orange,

A beautiful basket of Leicestershire-grown organic apples for sale at Picks Organic shop.

another apple produced on the Belvoir Estate. This eater has an intensely rich and aromatic flavour that gets rapidly stronger as it ripens. Another old cooker is the Queen Caroline, first produced at Ashby de la Zouch in 1820. It is not as sharp as most cookers, and reduces down to a creamy pulp when cooked.

There is also the unusual Syston Plum, a variety also known as the Golden Monarch. This plum is white when ripe, or rather a very pale yellow. It eats very well, but its main use was in the dying industry. Trainloads of the plums were shipped out of Syston in the mid-nineteenth century, but chemical dyes have now taken its place.

One late-comer to the range of varieties originating in the county was the Blaby Tomato, which was developed in the 1930s. The variety was developed on a large, commercial tomato farm growing huge amounts of the food under about four acres of glass, complete with heating pipes to force the plants to give an early crop. The farm was run by a Mr Shoult, who had moved to Leicestershire from Essex after the First World War. The tomato seems to have been a spontaneous mutation from the variety known as Anwell, which was the initial main crop at the farm.

The breed produces large fruits with a well-rounded flavour. For some reason the last fruit on each truss is misshapen and rarely ripens properly – it is known colloquially as 'the blue'.

The seasonal gluts of plant food were unpredictable and irregular. One year plum trees might produce barely any fruit at all, but the next the branches would be bent almost to the ground by the sheer weight of fruits. Finding ways to preserve these vast quantities of cheap, seasonally available foods was something of an obsession for rural folk. After all, the successful keeping of summer crops could mean the difference between survival and starvation in the winter and spring, before the new crops produced any food. March and April were traditionally the hungry months.

Most of the older methods of preserving foods have long since been superseded by more modern methods. Apples and other harder fruits were conventionally wrapped in paper, set on slatted trays so that they did not touch each other and stored in dark, well-aired sheds or barns. Most of these apples would survive for a few months, though some always spoiled. Other fruits were more suitable for drying, though they then had to be included into various dishes that made them rather more appetising than they would have been otherwise.

Of all the traditional ways of preserving foods only two have really survived: jams and pickles. Those continue to be popular not so much because they preserve food, but because they are tasty treats in their own right.

These days, of course, fruits and vegetables can be frozen, tinned or irradiated to make them last longer. And we have become almost blasé about crops being brought in by aircraft or refrigerated

A range of jams and pickles for sale at Pick's Organic shop.

ships from distant countries so that we can enjoy them when they are out of season here. Unlike our ancestors we are able to enjoy the recipes for consuming fruits and vegetables almost year round.

The twentieth century has brought one exciting innovation to the way vegetables are prepared in Leicestershire, raising to international prominence one local business of humble origins. The business in question was a butcher's shop in Leicester's High Street which had been founded in the 1880s by Henry Walker, a butcher from Mansfield. The company prospered and expanded, but in the 1940s it ran into difficulties due to the shortage of rationed meat. Keen to find work for his staff and a new product to sell, the then managing director, R.E. Gerrard, decided to start making potato crisps. The first batches were hand sliced and fried in deep saucepans, but the popularity of the new Walker's Crisps with the Leicester public soon led to an expansion and some more suitable, purpose-made equipment.

At this date, potato crisps were enjoying a boom in popularity due to two key inventions made in the 1930s. The first was the development of an air-tight packaging material that could be easily sealed shut by applying heat. This enabled potato crisps to stay fresh and tasty for several weeks after they were produced. The second was a method of applying powdered flavourings by tumbling the crisps in a drum that neither broke the crisps nor spoiled the flavours.

Armed with these two inventions, Walker's was soon able to produce crisps on a large scale and in several different flavours. Using the sealed bag, they could transport their products far beyond the confines of Leicester, secure in the knowledge that they would remain in good condition and fit to eat. During the 1960s and 1970s the two most popular flavours of crisp in Britain were 'Salt and Vinegar' and 'Cheese and Onion'. All other manufacturers put the Salt and Vinegar crisps into blue packets and Cheese and Onion into green packets. Walker's packaged their crisps the other way round and so made their products instantly recognisable.

Today Walker's is part of the larger PepsiCo food company. It has established itself as the market leader for snack foods in England and continues to expand as the quality of its foods remains undimmed.

## Plum Chutney

**Preparation time: 15 minutes**     **Cooking time: up to 90 minutes**

Now in my opinion a Melton Mowbray pork pie is perfection in itself, but a chap in the town told me that it tastes even better with this chutney on the side.

### Ingredients
1½lb plums, unripe if possible
8oz onion, chopped
8oz tomatoes, chopped
4lb brown sugar
1 teaspoon cayenne pepper
1 dessert spoon salt
1½ pts malt vinegar.

### Method
❖ Put all the ingredients into a saucepan and simmer gently until the mixture becomes thick and gloopy. This should take about an hour, but may take up to 90 minutes depending on the ripeness and quality of the plums and tomatoes. When cool, put into jars and seal down tightly.

## Beetroot Relish

**Preparation time: 15 minutes**     **Cooking time: About 30 minutes.**

This goes very well with Stilton cheese and crusty bread, but also goes well with fish.

### Ingredients
2lb beetroot, cooked, peeled and chopped
2lb cabbage, chopped
2 tablespoons grated horseradish
7 pts vinegar
8oz sugar
1 teaspoon pepper
1 tablespoon mustard
1 teaspoon salt

### Method
❖ Put all the ingredients into a saucepan and simmer for about 30 minutes. When cool, put into jars and seal down tightly.

# Mrs Comber's Sauce

**Preparation time: 40 minutes**     **Standing time: 15 days**

I wasn't quite sure where to put this recipe, but I really could not miss it out. I finally decided to put it in this chapter as it involves shallots and walnuts, but it really stands alone. The sauce has a curious history, which I will repeat to you as it was told by the Master of the Quorn Hunt in the 1920s and written down:

> Captain Charles Comber (born 1752), a member of the Quorn Hunt when on his way to Leicestershire stopped, as was his wont, to dine at The George at Bedford, then kept by a man named Harvey, where he ordered a steak, and when it was served, Comber requested Harvey to let his servant bring from his buggy a quart bottle which contained an admirable sauce. Comber poured some of it into his plate and having mixed it with the gravy of the steak he asked Harvey to taste it, and the host pronounced it to be a most excellent relish.
>
> 'Well Harvey,' said Comber, 'I shall leave the bottle with you to use till my return, only be careful to reserve enough for me.'
>
> On the next day Harvey had to provide a wedding dinner, and introduced the sauce which afforded such general satisfaction that several smaller parties were made up and the contents of the bottle were soon exhausted.
>
> In due course Captain Comber returned and having been told no more sauce remained, said 'Never mind, I can make some more from my mother's recipe and, by the by, I'll give you a copy of it.' He did so. Harvey made it in large quantities, sent it to different shops in London; advertised it as Harvey's Sauce and by its extensive sale realised a large income. He subsequently sold the recipe for an annuity of £400 a year.

Here is the recipe. I will admit that I have not made this myself, but I just could not resist the story.

## Ingredients

12 anchovies
1oz cayenne pepper
6 dessert spoons soy sauce
6 dessert spoons pickled walnut, chopped
3 bulbs (not cloves) garlic, peeled and chopped
1 teaspoon cochineal (or similar red food colouring)
2 shallots, peeled and chopped
1 gallon malt vinegar

## Method

❖ Chop the anchovies very finely.
❖ Add the cayenne pepper, soy sauce and walnuts
❖ Add the garlic, shallots and cochineal.
❖ Add the vinegar
❖ Let it stand for 14 days.
❖ Stir it well each morning and each evening.
❖ Pass the sauce through a jelly bag for 12 hours.
❖ Bottle and cork securely.

# Crab Apple Jelly

**Preparation time: 15 minutes**     **Cooking time: 50 minutes**     **Straining time: overnight**

There are not many things that you can usefully do with crab apples, but this is one of them. You will need a jelly bag, which not everybody has, but it is worth the effort for the end result.

## Ingredients

Crab apples, as many as you like
1 lemon
Sugar

## Method

❖ Wash the crab apples, but don't peel them, and place into a large, heavy bottomed pan.

❖ Add water to just cover the crab apples.

❖ Bring to the boil and simmer until the fruit is reduced to a pulp.

❖ Pour into a jelly bag and leave to drain into a fresh saucepan for at least 12 hours. Do not touch the bag.

❖ Discard the fruit pulp.

❖ Measure the liquid.

❖ Add 1lb of sugar for every pint of liquid.

❖ Add the juice of the lemon.

❖ Heat gently until the sugar is dissolved, then bring to the boil.

❖ Boil for about 20 minutes until the jelly sets when a small amount is put on a cold plate.

❖ Allow to cool, then put into jars and seal tightly.

# Raspberry and Rose Pannacotta

**Serves 4**     **Preparation time: 20 minutes**     **Chilling time: 3 hours minimum**

This delicate dessert can be made very quickly and prepared well in advance, even a day or two before hand. If fresh raspberries are not available you can use frozen.

Raspberry Pannacotta uses some of the finest fruits that Leicestershire has to offer.

## Ingredients

8fl oz skimmed milk
8fl oz double cream
5fl oz raspberry and rose
cordial (available from Belvoir
Fruit Farms)
Gelatin to set 1pt of liquid
2½oz caster sugar
8oz raspberries
1oz icing sugar

## Method

❖ Prepare the Gelatin as per the packet instructions.
❖ Pour the cream and sugar into a pan and heat gently until the sugar has dissolved.
❖ Bring momentarily to the boil, then remove from the heat.
❖ Stir in the Gelatin and 3fl oz of cordial, whisk until thoroughly mixed.
❖ Leave to cool for about 10 minutes.
❖ Stir in the skimmed milk and pour into 4 ramekins.
❖ Chill in a fridge for at least 3 hours, or until set.
❖ Meanwhile, purée half the raspberries with the icing sugar then sieve.
❖ Mix the purée with the remaining raspberries.
❖ Place each ramekin on a plate, pile on the raspberries and purée.
❖ Top with fresh mint, if available, and serve.

# Pinot Grigio, Raspberry and Rose Jelly

| Serves 2 | Preparation time: 10 minutes | Chilling time: 4 hours or until set |

This lovely little jelly is ideal for a romantic night in for two, but if you plan to serve it at a dinner just increase the quantities. Fresh raspberries are best for this summer dish, but frozen can be used if necessary. If you have got any sense, you will drink the rest of the bottle of Pinot Grigio with dinner.

## Ingredients

Gelatin to set ½ pt liquid
1½oz sugar
2fl oz water
1/3 bottle Pinot Grigio blush
3fl oz raspberry and rose
cordial (available from Belvoir
Fruit Farms)
Juice of ½ lemon
½lb fresh raspberries

## Method

❖ Prepare the Gelatin as per packet instructions.
❖ Place the sugar and water in a saucepan.
❖ Heat gently while stirring until the sugar is dissolved, then bring to the boil and simmer for 2 minutes.
❖ Remove from the heat.
❖ Add the Gelatin and whisk until dissolved.
❖ Add the pinot grigio, cordial and lemon juice and stir well.
❖ Meanwhile, place several raspberries in the bottom of two wine glasses.
❖ Pour over just enough of the jelly to cover the raspberries.
❖ Chill in a fridge until set.
❖ Add the rest of the jelly to fill the glasses almost to the brim.
❖ Chill in the fridge until set.
❖ Serve with the remaining raspberries.

Pinot Grigio and raspberries form the base of a truly scrumptious dessert recipe from Leicestershire.

# Blackcurrant Fool with Shortbreads

| Serves 4 | Preparation time: 30 minutes | Cooking time: nil |

This magnificent dessert is bound to impress. Ideally you should use lavender sugar, but this is not always available so caster sugar will do just as well. If you want to make your own lavender sugar, push a couple of sprigs of lavender deep into a bag of sugar, wrap tightly with clingfilm and leave in a cool place for a week or so. If you want to be extra flash you could bake your own shortbreads, but high quality shortbreads can be bought in most supermarkets these days and save a lot of trouble.

## Ingredients

8oz blackcurrants
4fl oz Blackcurrant cordial (available from Belvoir Fruit Farms)
1oz caster sugar
5fl oz custard, made firmly and left to chill
5fl oz Greek style yoghurt
4fl oz whipping cream, whipped to a solid consistency
12 round shortbread biscuits
1oz icing sugar

## Method

❖ Place the blackcurrants, cordial and sugar in a saucepan.
❖ Heat gently until the sugar has dissolved, then bring to the boil and simmer for 4 minutes.
❖ Leave the blackcurrant mixture to cool.
❖ Meanwhile, mix the yoghurt and custard together.
❖ Add two tablespoons full of juice from the blackcurrant mix.
❖ Gently fold the yoghurt mixture into the whipped cream so that it retains its stiffness and becomes a fool.
❖ Immediately before serving, put the dessert together by repeating the following process on each of four plates. Placing a biscuit on a plate, add a spoonful of fool, then a second biscuit, then another spoonful of fool and top with a third biscuit. Sprinkle liberally with icing sugar and then carefully drizzle over some of the liquid from the blackcurrant mixture. Serve with the blackcurrant mixture spooned on to the side of each plate. Garnish with a sprig of fresh mint, if available.

The completed dessert of Blackcurrant Fool has shortbread biscuits layered with fool and topped by icing sugar and blackcurrant sauce.

*Nine*

# WASHING IT DOWN

Drinking in Leicestershire has always been as much a pleasure as a necessity. Humans need a regular and relatively pure intake of water to remain healthy. In prehistoric times the many streams, rivers and springs of the county were more than enough to provide the liquid refreshment that the people craved.

As the population grew, however, it began to be noticed that drinking water from some sources led to stomach ache, intestinal problems and sickness. At the time, nobody understood about contaminated water and the need for efficient sewage disposal. They did, however, have eyes to see and brains with which to interpret what they saw. Some sources of water were avoided, others became highly esteemed.

Some time before the Romans came, and perhaps as early as 2000 BC, somebody noticed that there was one way of processing water that usually purified it and made it safe to drink. Rather conveniently this process also made it very tasty and slightly alcoholic. The new process was to brew the water into beer. At the time nobody understood what it was about brewing beer that made stale or suspect water wholesome, all they knew was that it worked.

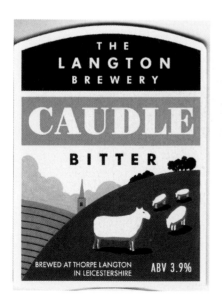

One of the bitters brewed at the Langton Brewery in Thorpe Langton is named after the nearby Caudle Hill. Beer has been brewed in Leicestershire for at least 4,000 years and probably much longer.

There are numerous variations on the brewing process, each producing a different sort of beer, but the basic technique has not altered in 4,000 years. The basic ingredients are malt and water. The malt is usually barley, though wheat and other grains have been used. The grains are wetted and kept in a warm room for a few days until they begin to sprout The seed at this stage naturally converts the stored starch – which is the main component of flour – into sugars that can be used by the growing plant. The sprouting grain is then rolled to break open the grains and expose the sugar.

The malt is then mixed with hot water and simmered, or mashed, for up to two hours. The water, now termed wort, is drained off, taking with it the sugars and various flavouring elements from the malt. The wort is then brought to the boil, before being cooled to a lukewarm temperature, at which point the yeast is added. The yeast converts the sugars into alcohol, and also throws up a sediment made up of tiny grains of insoluble matter. This sinks to the bottom of the fermenting tank, as does the yeast when it no longer has enough sugar on which to feed. The process may take a couple of days, or several months depending on the type of yeast used and other factors.

The beer is then racked off from the fermenting tank into barrels, or more recently into bottles. In some cases a short, limited secondary fermentation may then take place which results in the beer becoming slightly bubbly, and small amount of sediment forming in the barrel.

Although our prehistoric ancestors did not understand how brewing beer purified the water, it is clear that it was the prolonged boiling of the water at two different stages that killed off the bugs and infections that were in the water. These days beer is almost always produced to be an enjoyable alcoholic beverage, but in centuries past its prime use was often as a healthy drink. The alcoholic content of beer might have been as high as 3 per cent by volume, but the vast majority of beer was much weaker. The malt was used many times over, each time producing a brew progressively weaker in alcoholic terms, but always as healthy as the first. The so-called small beer was so weak as to be almost non-alcoholic. This was probably just as well, for it was drunk in prodigious quantities in medieval towns and cities.

Just some of the range of beers produced by the Belvoir Brewery. Leicestershire has several smaller breweries producing a wide range of beers.

Over the years a wide variety of ingredients have been added to beer to improve its flavour. Herbs such as rosemary and sage were popular, but so were fruit juices of various kinds. Honey was often mixed in to make the beer sweeter and egg yolks were put in to make it a healthy drink for invalids and the elderly. It was not until the fifteenth century that hops began to be added. These made beer bitter, as it is usually today, but also improved its keeping properties. Today hopped beer is the usual form.

In the past, most beer was brewed in the home, and home brewing kits are today available and sell well. Most people, however, prefer to drink beer that has been brewed by experts in breweries, and in Leicestershire there is a good variety of breweries to choose from. These are listed in the final section of this book, but far and away the largest and oldest of the Leicestershire breweries is Everards. The company was founded in 1849 by William Everard, the third son of a prosperous farmer from Thurlaston. One of William's brothers moved to Australia, another went to China to make money as a tea merchant, while a cousin ran the local pub. It may have been the profits made by cousin Thomas that inspired William to invest his money in a brewery in Leicester. He was to run the ever expanding business until his death in 1893. By then, Everards was an established part of life in Leicestershire.

Since 1982 the brewery has been situated on a modern, purpose-built brewery at Narborough. There the company still adheres to the dictum laid down by founder William Everard: 'No effort should be found wanting in the production and supply of genuine ale of the first-rate quality'. The company is now not only a brewer, but also the owner of a spreading estate of pubs, hotels and other premises. The advertising side of the business has been particularly innovative in recent years, winning several awards, and the beers go from strength to strength.

When prehistoric people in Leicestershire wanted to drink alcohol they were more likely to drink mead than beer. Made from honey mixed with water and left to ferment in pottery tubs, mead was in Celtic society reserved for warriors and nobles. It retained its aristocratic image into Roman times, but then was superseded by the new and more fashionable wine. In Leicestershire, mead never regained its snob value, nor its popularity. It was drunk in medieval times, but was never very popular and remains a novelty drink.

Wine, on the other hand, is still both drunk and made in Leicestershire as it was in Roman times. The drink seems to have been first made in the Caucasus Mountains of southern Russia around 8,000 years ago. It was then primarily a way of preserving the sugars and minerals found in grapes to be consumed in the winter. By 2000 BC, however, the making of wine had spread across the Mediterranean basin and was being treated as an enjoyable alcoholic beverage rather than as a way of preserving grapes.

The drink has had something of a chequered history in Leicestershire, coming and going with the changing climate. As the Romans pulled out in AD 410, the climate of Britain was getting colder and wetter. Indeed the changing climate may have been one reason for the gradual collapse in Roman prosperity that in turn led to the fall of the empire. By around AD 500 it was impossible to grow grapes in Britain and wine died out as a drink. It is mentioned a few times in written records during the centuries that followed, but only ever as a rare import.

By AD 950 the climate was getting warmer and drier again. Grapes could be grown more easily in northern Europe than before and so the drink became cheaper and more available. In AD 982 a royal tax was imposed on its import for the first time and a century later vineyards were again being planted in southern England. Records of vineyards in Leicestershire are rare, but Leicester Abbey certainly owned vineyards that seem to have been in the county.

**Above:** David and Jane Bates enjoy some of their award-winning wine at their Welland Valley Vineyard.

**Above right:** Grapes being harvested at the Welland Valley Vineyard. The cultivation of grapes has come and gone in Leicestershire over the past 2,000 years as the climate has alternately warmed and cooled.

**Right:** A bottle of the prestigious Tickled Pink sparkling wine produced at Welland Valley Vineyard.

Around 1350 the climate again began to shift and entered a period of chilly weather that once more drove vineyards out of Leicestershire. The climate began to swing back again in the nineteenth century and by the mid-twentieth century it was again possible to grow grapes in the county. In the closing decades of the twentieth century commercial vineyards were planted and by the opening decade of the twenty-first century they were making wine every bit as good as those imported from the continent.

Not all drinks made in Leicestershire have been alcoholic. Very early on it was discovered that boiling fruits in water not only created a tasty, fruity drink but also made the water as safe to drink as if it had been made into beer. These various fruit waters have long since fallen out of favour, but they were the inspiration for the fruit cordials and other fruit-based drinks that continue to be made in the county to this day.

*Ten*

# LIST OF SUPPLIERS

The following list of producers and suppliers of quality, traditional foods in Leicestershire is not exhaustive. There are many dozens of small shops, producers and craftsmen (and craftswomen) who are busily turning out truly delicious products all over the county. I have not, however, been able to get hold of contact details for all of these enterprises, or have not personally sampled their wares and so feel unable to recommend them. If you would like to recommend any producer for inclusion in a future edition of this book, please contact me via the publisher.

## Meat

**A.E. TAYLOR & SONS**

This family run butcher's shop has been in the Taylor family since the 1870s and with a new generation ready to take over from the current Mr Taylor, it looks set to remain supplying meat to the good folk of Bottesford for some years to come.

Taylor's supplies everything that the discerning shopper could want from a butcher's. In addition to the normal cuts of meat and poultry, the shop sells pies, haslet and sausages prepared by the family. Cooked meats are also on offer, together with locally sourced hams and tongue. The Stilton cheese comes from Colston Basset. The beef comes from Titlemouse Hall Farm at Muston, barely a mile from the shop, while the lamb and pork is also sourced from local farms – some of which have been supplying Taylor's for generations.

This is one of the very few butcher's which still slaughter on the premises. The yard at the rear contains not just the slaughterhouse, but also extensive storage facilities where the meat is hung. Mr Taylor undertakes slaughtering for local small holders as well as to supply his own shop. He reckons to process an average of two cattle and twenty sheep each week. The shop is open Monday to Saturday. Telephone orders are taken.

A butcher's as it should be.

**A.E. Taylor & Sons**
The Cross
Bottesford
Leicestershire
LE13 0AA          **Tel:** 01949 842319

The Blackbrook meat business is based at the family run farm of Spring Barrow Lodge Farm on the edge of the Charnwood Forest. The livestock are farmed extensively to produce a stress free environment which is better for the animals and produces better quality meat, whilst also farming in the most environmentally sustainable way. All the livestock come from native breeds and remain on the farm for their entire lifetime.

The lamb comes from Jacob and Suffolk cross-bred sheep which are raised on the farm and grass finished. The meat is hung for two weeks to result in unrivalled flavour and tenderness. The pork comes from a rare breed of Welsh pigs which boats less fat than most pork while producing an intense succulence. The beef comes exclusively from the herd of Longhorn cattle that are allowed to mature slowly, resulting in excellent marbling which creates an intense and old-fashioned flavour. The beef is hung for up to four weeks, resulting in amazingly tender meat and superior eating quality of all cuts.

**Blackbrook Traditional Meats**
Spring Barrow Lodge Farm
Grace Dieu            **Tel:**       01509 503276
Leicestershire        **Email:**     info@blackbrook-longhorns.com
LE67 5UT              **Website:**   www.blackbrook-longhorns.com

This farm produces what might be termed 'tame game' in form of farmed bison and venison. All animals are grazed free range on the 100 acre farm. The animals eat grass in summer, with their diet being supplemented by natural foods such as hay, potatoes and apples in winter. Animal welfare is of the greatest importance at Bouverie Lodge and is constant through the husbandry process. It is extended to the slaughter of the animals which is done on-site to minimise stress. The venison is a tender and finely grained meat with virtually no fat. Bison is significantly higher in protein, but lower in fat and calories than any other meat – including poultry and fish. Bison can be cooked as if it were beef, but gives a sweeter, richer flavour. Cooking hints and recipes are available from Bouverie Lodge.

Bouverie Lodge began in 2001 with a herd of just six bison, but has grown rapidly to become one of the market leaders in bison and deer meat in the UK. It now boasts a herd of some eighty bison and over 100 deer. Visitors are welcome to the farm to view the animals in the fields and to purchase produces from the on-site shop. Products may also be purchased at assorted farmers markets around the county.

**Bouverie Lodge,**
Nottingham Road
Nether Broughton
Melton Mowbray        **Tel:**       01664 822114
Leicestershire        **Email:**     info@bisons.org
LE14 3EX              **Website:**   www.bisons.org

Brockleby's sells through its farm shop in Asfordby Hill, Melton Mowbray and at shows, events and markets across the East Midlands, up to twenty-six per month. Brockleby's Farm Shop opened in April 2005 and is a showcase for regionally-produced food and drink. Its sourcing policy is Leicestershire first, regional second, supplemented with a range of organic and speciality foods. As well as local meat, it has a delicatessen selling local cheeses, cooked meats, brawn, sausages and burgers. It stocks locally brewed beers, organic wines, locally milled flour, regionally grown vegetables. It also sells locally made chocolates and cakes. It has a range of gluten-free and dairy-free foods. There are more than 1,000 products on sale at Brockleby's Farm Shop. Staff are trained in the provenance of products and encouraged to share their knowledge with customers.

Brockleby's was conceived in 2003, retailing locally sourced meat, sausages and burgers across the East Midlands through shows, events and farmers' markets. Brockleby's Farm Shop opened in 2005 and is now a busy retail outlet, signed on all major routes to Melton Mowbray. It welcomes an estimated 60,000 visitors a year. Brockleby's is the only producer of an organic Melton Mowbray pork pie.

The business was built on the principle of 'Food With Provenance'. The shop and retail stalls at shows are only the front for a much larger team that includes farmers, butchers, bakers, retailers and wholesalers. So the food, from field to fork, is always under their control. The business seeks to tell customers who raised the pigs used to make the sausages, and the animals for the beef in the pies.

Products and ingredients are sourced very carefully. The Saddleback pigs used in Brockleby's pies, for example are raised by Richard Mee, of Oakley Grange Farm, Hathern, and lead happy, natural lives. In fact, all the livestock in the Brockleby's food chain is reared in a natural, free-ranging environment. Where possible, organic ingredients are used, all the pork and beef in the pies is organic, as is the unbleached flour used for the pastry.

Brockleby's pies are hand-raised, hand-filled and inspected by eye. The pastry is made from scratch using organic, unbleached flour milled at Whissendine Windmill. A team of artisan pie-makers work in full view of the public in the shop's open plan kitchen. The Brockleby's pie range includes: Organic Melton Mowbray Pork Pie, Organic Picnic Pie, Longhorn Steak Parcel, Longhorn Beef Pie, Moroccan Lamb Pie, Shepherd's Delight, Free Range Chicken Pie, Poacher's Game Pie, Summer Isles Salmon Pie and Suzy's Apple Pie. For the summer picnic spread, there is a quiche range and free range scotch eggs. The ready-meal range includes: Longhorn Beef Lasagna; Longhorn Beef and Melton Red Ale; Wild Venison and Seasonal Berries; Sweet and Sour Rare Breed Pork; Free Range Chicken Tikka Masala and Hebridean Lamb Tagine.

## Brockleby's Food

| | | |
|---|---|---|
| Asfordby Hill | **Tel:** | 01664 813200 |
| Leicestershire | **Email:** | ian.jalland@brocklebys.co.uk |
| LE14 3QU | **Website:** | www.brocklebys.co.uk |

Dickinson & Morris are best known for their magnificent Melton Mowbray pork pies, made in the traditional method and with the finest of ingredients. Their premises at Ye Olde Pork Pie Shoppe lives up to its name by having a room devoted to shelf after shelf of these delicious pies. They come in four sizes: Mini (2oz), Individual (the original at 6oz), Large (1lb) and Extra Large (2lb).

The shop also sells a wide variety of cheeses, biscuits, cakes, pickles and chutneys. The Melton Hunt Cake is the most prized of the cakes. It was originally made in the 1850s for members of the local hunt to eat whilst out foxhunting. The cake is still made using the original recipe combining the finest ingredients; sultanas, currants, muscavado sugar, butter, fresh eggs, cherries and almonds, all enhanced with Caribbean rum. These products are made up into luxury hampers for the Christmas trade and can be ordered online via the website or by post.

The Sausage Shop, next door to the pie shop, offers a stunning range of homemade sausages including: pork sausage, pork chipolata, Rutland sausage, Lincolnshire sausage, Toulouse sausage, Melton smokey sausage, pork and leek sausage, chestnut stuffing sausage, bacon sausage and smokey bacon sausage as well as a range of seasonal offerings and some one-off specials from time to time.

**Dickinson & Morris**
Ye Olde Pork Pie Shoppe
8–10 Nottingham Street
Melton Mowbray          **Tel:**      01664 482068
Leicestershire          **Email:**    dickinson&morris@porkpie.co.uk
LE13 1NW                **Website:** www.porkpie.co.uk

## MARK PATRICK HIGH CLASS BUTCHER

A quality family butcher.

85 Sibson Road,
Birstall,                **Tel:**      0116 267 4341
Leicester                **Email:**    info@markpatrickbutchers.co.uk
LE4 4NB                  **Website:** www.markpatrickbutchers.co.uk

## STEPHEN MORRIS BUTCHER

A magnificent town centre butcher that takes phone orders.

26/27 High Street
Loughborough
Leicestershire           **Tel:**      01509 215260
LE11 2PZ                 **Email:**    contact@stephenmorrisbutchers.co.uk

## CHAPPELL'S FINE FOODS LTD

A maker of traditional – and very tasty – Melton Mowbray pork pies.

61 Chartwell Drive
Wigston
Leicestershire
LE18 2FS

**Tel:** 0116 2812087
**Email:** sue@meltonmowbrayporkpies.com

## DAVID COX BUTCHERS

Mr Cox's shop is based in the heart of the Vale of Belvoir near Melton Mowbray. He has been a licensed butcher for over thirty years and offers refrigerated deliveries to the surrounding area. Alongside all the quality meats you might expect, Mr Cox also stocks Long Clawson Best Blue Stilton, Bailey's pork pies and a wide variety of home-cooked meats, cakes and pastries.

27 Main Street
Stathern
Melton Mowbray
Leicestershire
LE14 4HW

**Tel:** 01949 861066

## KINGSTON BROOK FARM

235 Narrow Lane
Wymeswold
Leicestershire
LE12 6SD

**Tel:** 01509 881098

## F. BAILEY & SON

A leading maker of Melton Mowbray pork pies.

Station Road
Upper Broughton
Leicestershire
LE14 3BQ

**Tel:** 01664 822216

## NORTHFIELD FARM

Northfield Farm straddles the Rutland Leicestershire border midway between Oakham and Melton Mowbray. The main herd is of Dexter cattle, a small, short-legged cow of ancient origin, believed to come from Ireland. The breed is famous for its prodigious quantities of creamy milk and truly succulent beef. The farm also has a herd of White Park Cattle, one of the oldest British breeds that dates back at least 800 years.

Northfield Farm Limited has been accredited as a butcher by the Rare Breeds Survival Trust since 1997 as a tribute to the quality of the produce and the principles according to which the livestock is bred and reared.

The farm shop opened in 1997 and now sources products from around fifty suppliers. It also deals in game and stocks truly free range Geese and Turkeys for Christmas. As well as the core business of meat, Northfield Farm also sells a range of British cheeses, honeys, breads, vegetables, locally brewed bottled beers, and much more.

**Northfield Farm**
Whissendine Lane
Cold Overton          **Tel:**     01664 474271
Rutland               **Email:**   marc@northfieldfarm.com
LE15 7QF              **Website:** www.northfieldfarm.com

## THOMPSON FAMILY BUTCHER

Thompson's Family Butchers shop was established over eighteen years ago and is conveniently situated right in the centre of Melton Mowbray. It is a family run business, run by Diana and Ivan Thompson. Diana makes all the sausages from her own recipes. These include: old English, plain pork, tomato, beef and venison. She also cooks all their hams and makes their haslet. Thompson's Butchers supply a number of prestige local hotels and restaurants already in and around Melton Mowbray.

**Thompson Butchers**
10 Marketplace
Melton Mowbray
Leicestershire        **Website:** www.thebestof.co.uk/melton%20mowbray/25948/1/1/
LE13 1XD                         the_best_of.aspx#Reviews


# Cheese and Dairy Products

## GOPSALL FRESH FARMHOUSE ICE CREAM

The Thorp family have farmed at Culloden Farm for over seventy years. The brothers Tony and Norman now have a herd of about 100 Frisian cows grazing on the lush pastures. All calves are allowed to suckle naturally from their mothers before being added to the dairy or the beef herd.

The ice cream is produced on the farm, using local ingredients and flavours whenever possible. The ice creams can be bought at the farm and from a number of local outlets. Deliveries can be arranged in the county, or for larger quantities elsewhere in the UK. The ice cream is packaged into 120ml tubs, 500ml tubs and 4.5 litre tubs.

The more popular flavours are almost always available, including: Vanilla, Chunky Chocolate, Mint Choc Chip, Apple Crumble, Raspberry Pavolova, Woodland Fruits, Mango and Whisky & Ginger. At Christmas the two flavours of Plum & Brandy and Christmas Pud are best sellers, and other seasonal flavours are produced through the year.

For those interested in the arts, Gopsall Hall (now demolished) was where the composer George Handel was staying as the guest of Charles Jennens when in 1742 he composed his great work *The Messiah*. He also composed the hymn *Rejoice the Lord is King* while here, creating the tune while seated in the Temple folly, which still stands on the estate.

**Gopsall Ice Cream**
Culloden Farm
Twycross
Leicestershire          **Tel:**        01530 272000
CV9 3QJ                 **Email:**      thorpbrothers@btconnect.com

## LUBCLOUD DAIRY

This is a family run organic dairy farm overlooking the picturesque vale of Charley in the beautiful Charnwood Forest, which also offers bed and breakfast accommodation. The milk is pasteurised and bottled in the on-site dairy, meaning that milk can be supplied fresher and faster. The pasture land at Lubcloud is entirely free of artificial fertilisers, pesticides or herbicides, allowing Lubcloud to produce milk to the highest organic standards of the Soil Association. The grasses and plants have naturally high levels of trace elements, vitamins and no harmful chemical residues. The few additional feeds that are used are fully traceable and non-GM. For those taking advantage of the B&B facilities, the Farmhouse was built in the 1700's and has been extended several times over the centuries. You can still see some of the original features from the Victorian period in the hallway, namely a row of servant bells, fireplaces and a red and white tiled floor.

**The Lubcloud Dairy**
Charley Road
Oaks in Charnwood
Loughbrough          **Tel:**        01509 505055
Leicestershire       **Email:**      Info@lubcloudfarm.co.uk
LE12 9YA             **Website:** www.lubcloudfarm.co.uk

## LEICESTERSHIRE HANDMADE CHEESE CO.

This small dairy is based on Sparkenhoe Farm where cheeses were made in the traditional way from 1795 until 1956. The craft has now been revived by David and Jo Clarke who use milk from their herd of 150 pedigree Holstein-Frisians. The prime product is the Sparkenhoe Red Leicester, the only Red Leicester cheese to be made in the traditional way. In 2007, it was voted the Best British Raw Milk Cheese by the Specialist Cheesemakers trade organisation. The cheese is produced in traditional 20lb and 40lb wheels and is available from a range of stockists.

David manages the herd of over 150 pedigree Holstein-Frisian cows. The cows are fed on the farm's lush pastures and calving takes place all year round to keep the milk supply as consistent as possible. David and Jo started making 'Sparkenhoe', a traditional Leicester cheese in November 2005. They use the milk produced from their own cows and this is pumped straight from the parlour directly into the cheese vat ready to make the cheese.

The milk from the previous day's milking is pumped across from the parlour to the cheese room at 4 a.m. An old recipe discovered by Jo and David is then followed and traditional rennet added before annatto is then added to give the cheese its rich orange colour. Annatto is a natural plant dye obtained from a South American bush. The curds and whey are then scalded gently before being separated, the curds are then cut into blocks and turned to release further whey. The curds are finally put through the mill and salt is added. The cheese is put into moulds and pressed for twenty-four hours, turned and pressed for a further twenty-four hours. The cheeses are bound in cloth and lard and matured for four months in the store at 10°C.

**Leicestershire**
**Handmade Cheese Co.**
Sparkenhoe Farm
Upton                          **Tel:**      01455 213863
Leicestershire                 **Email:**    info@leicestershirecheese.co.uk
CV13 6JX                       **Website:**  www.leicestershirecheese.co.uk

## WEBSTER'S DAIRY

One of the more traditional family dairies producing Stilton cheese the way it should be produced, Webster's Dairy is located in idyllic rural surroundings in the hamlet of Saxelbye. Webster's has been producing Stilton cheese for the past 150 years in a row of seventeenth-century cottages. Webster's view making Stilton as both a passion and a skill. Every step of the lengthy process is overseen by people who have been cheesemakers most of their working lives. The company produces Blue Shropshire cheese as well as the traditional Blue Stilton. The dairy shop is open during office hours on weekdays and on Saturday and Sunday mornings. Products may also be ordered by post, see the website for details.

**Webster's Dairy**
Saxelbye
Melton Mowbray                 **Tel:**      01664 812223
Leicestershire                 **Email:**    m.callow@webstersdairy.co.uk
LE14 3PH                       **Website:**  www.webstersdairy.co.uk

## TUXFORD AND TEBBUTT CHEESEMAKERS

This small dairy produces both Stilton and Red Leicester cheese.

**The Cheese Company**
**Ltd**
Thorpe End
Melton Mowbray                 **Tel:**      01664 502911
Leicestershire                 **Email:**    exportsales@cheese.co.uk
LE13 1RB                       **Website:**  www.tuxfordandtebbutt.com

Long Clawson Dairy was founded in 1911 when twelve farmers from the Vale of Belvoir formed a co-operative to produce Stilton cheese in the village of Long Clawson. Today it has fifty-six producing members from thirty-nine farms supplying thirty-eight million litres of milk per year. The company now operates from three sites. In Long Clawson itself is the Head Office, Stilton Production Unit, Packing & Distribution centres. At Harby is a storage facility where the Stilton is matured and graded prior to being sent back to Clawson for packing and despatch. The Harby site was opened in 1985 by HRH The Prince of Wales. The Bottesford site handles the production of blended cheese. It was opened as a dedicated blended facility in 1979 following the launch of the Windsor Red cheese.

The company produces an awesome range of cheeses. The heart of the business remains the strong cheeses: Blue Stilton, Blue Shropshire & Blue Vinney along with the mellower Mature Blue Stilton. White Stilton is made in the same way as Blue Stilton except that no blue mould is added to the milk. There are many wonderful savoury cheeses such as the Cotswold, Huntsman, Charnwood and Fiery Mex. Rather different are the fruit blends. These are all based on creamy White Stilton with added fruits, such as lemon peel, apricot, strawberries, blueberries or even mango & ginger.

Long Clawson Dairy cheeses are widely available in local shops, but also in supermarkets across the country.

Long Clawson
Melton Mowbray          **Tel:**      01664 822332
Leicestershire          **Email:**    enquiries@clawson.co.uk
LE14 4PJ                **Website:**  www.clawson.co.uk/uk_home.asp


# Retailers & Shops

## PICK'S ORGANIC FARM SHOP

Pick's is a family run farm and has been producing organic meat and vegetables since 1999. Their crops are grown and animals reared without the use of artificial pesticides or fertilisers, growth hormones or routine antibiotics. Crops are grown in a way that enhances the environment, maintains the quality of the soil and does not harm wild life.

The organic pork comes from a herd of Gloucester Old Spot pigs who spend the summer months rooting in the the fields and come inside only during the severest winter weather. Some of the pork is cured into bacon, so gammon joints are available, while other cuts are processed into sausages and chipolatas.

The organic beef comes from a herd of Dexter cattle. The meat is hung in a small, local slaughterhouse for up to three weeks before being jointed and returned to Pick's for retail sale as joints or burgers.

The organic poultry is free range and come from flocks of White Ross Cobbs which are plump and tender birds. There are also organic turkeys, guinea fowl, ducks and geese. Eggs from the chickens are collected twice daily and sold in the shop. Subject to seasonal availability, the organic duck eggs are also for sale in the shop.

The farm shop is open seven days a week, 9 a.m. to 6 p.m. Boxes of organic fruit and vegetables are delivered in the county and nearby areas in three sizes. See website for details.

### Pick's Organic Farm Shop
The Cottage
Hamilton Grounds

| | | |
|---|---|---|
| Barkby Thorpe | **Tel:** | 0116 269 3548 |
| Leicestershire | **Email:** | nicky@picksorganic.co.uk |
| LE7 3QF | **Website:** | www.picksorganic.co.uk |

# *Drinks*

## THE BELVOIR BREWERY

Colin Brown set up the original Belvoir Brewery in 1995 with equipment that was mostly new, but included some recovered from traditional cask ale breweries across the country. In 2007 the brewery moved, with the help of a DEFRA grant, to a purpose built brewery and visitor centre in Old Dalby. Colin uses only time-honoured brewing methods and the finest malt and hops – including hops from Worcester and malted English barley.

The Belvoir Brewery is open every afternoon and some evenings (see website for up to date details). The shop sells beers in a range of sizes from bottles to small barrels, along with a range of locally produced foods ideal to enjoy with a glass of beer. Belvoir Brewery merchandise is also available along with gift packs and clothing. The on-site restaurant offers a wide variety of dishes and is available for functions. Tours of the brewery are available by appointment.

### The Belvoir Brewery
Crown Park
Station Road

| | | |
|---|---|---|
| Old Dalby | **Tel:** | 01664 823 455 |
| Leicestershire | **Email:** | colin@belvoirbrewery.co.uk |
| LE14 3NQ | **Website:** | www.belvoirbrewery.co.uk |

## BELVOIR FRUIT FARMS

Belvoir Fruit Farm was simply that – a fruit farm – until in 1984 owner Lord John Manners' wife Mary began making elderflower cordial for her family, using flowers picked from the hedgerows around the farm. Friends and neighbours would beg steal or 'borrow' bottles until the popularity of the product saw the production of a few cases of the elderflower in small hand-made batches which were sold in local shops.

By the late 1980s, Lord John was producing a range of cordials using soft fruits from the Farm's fruit fields, pressed in an antique French wine press. Organic production began with the planting of ninety acres of organic elderflowers in the spring of 1995. Nestling in the beautiful Vale of Belvoir, the elder bushes grow very well and produced the first commercial harvest of flowers in 1998. Elderflower cordial was then followed by other organic cordials, and production is still expanding today.

The business is now run by Peverel Manners, son of the founders, who continues to use fruit from local fruit farmers and highly reputed importers of, for instance, fresh ginger and fresh lemon grass. The fruits and flowers are squeezed, crushed, pressed, cooked or infused on-site to keep their freshness and taste.

**Belvoir Fruit Farms**

| | | |
|---|---|---|
| Belvoir | **Tel:** | 01476 870286 |
| Leicestershire | **Email:** | info@belvoirfruitfarms.co.uk |
| NG32 1PB | **Website:** | www.belvoirfruitfarms.co.uk |

## THE LANGTON BREWERY

This small craft brewery began life in November 1999 when Derek Hewitt and Alistair Chapman were sitting in the Bell Inn, East Langton, complaining to each other about the declining quality of beer and the number of small breweries that were closing down. At the time Alistair was landlord of the Bell, while Derek was on the point of retiring after spending forty-four years as a banker. They decided to do something about the problem.

After buying some second-hand brewing equipment, Derek and Alistair began producing beer and selling it at the Bell Inn. They decided to base their new business on the philosophy of 'Producing traditional ale free from additives and using local water, English malt and English hops'. Their first brew was dubbed 'Caudle', after a local hill, and the rather stronger 'Bowler's', named in tribute to the link between the pub and the village cricket team.

Since then the brewery has expanded in terms of both size and output. It is now based at Grange Farm, thanks to Richard and Jim Mount, and a third partner has been taken on in the shape of David Dyson. The range of beers has been expanded to include bottle-conditioned beers as well as a number of one-off brews for special events, beer festivals and local restaurants and pubs. The range currently includes:

Caudle Bitter: 3.9% ABV. An easy drinking beer close to a pale ale, but with a traditional bitter taste.
Bowler Bitter: 4.8% ABV. A strong traditional ale with a deep red colour and hoppy scent.
Inclined Plane: 4.2% ABV. A straw-coloured bitter with a citrus scent and long hoppy finish – a lovely refreshing drink.

Other beers are available at different times of year. The Festive Frolic is, for instance, produced at Christmas.

Langton Brewery beers can be purchased at a number of shops in the county, or can be purchased directly from the brewery. Draught beers are sold in 10 litre or 20 litre polypins, or in 9 gallon casks. Bottled beers are sold individually or by the case.

**The Langton Brewery**
Grange Farm
Thorpe Langton
Leicestershire
LE16 7TU           **Tel:**      07840 532826

## MELTON MOWBRAY HEDGEROW LIQUEURS

Rachel Birch launched her business in 2004 producing just one drink, Melton Mowbray Sloe Gin. The drink has a distinctive warm and fruity flavour to complement any occasion. It is traditionally drunk neat as a winter warmer, or after dinner to complement cheese. In the summer it may be mixed with tonic water or lemonade to make a refreshing thirst quencher.

Rachel now also produces Wild Damson Whisky and Blackberry Vodka, all at 25 per cent alcohol by volume. The damson drink is a must try for the whisky lover. The rich and striking flavour of the damsons complements the heart-warming intensity of the whisky. The blackberry vodka is a subtle but powerful liqueur that allows the unique flavour and aroma of the blackberries to prevail.

She also hand-makes the delicious Melton Mowbray Sloe Gin Truffles, using the sloes that are extracted from the Sloe Gin. These fruits are then blended with a white chocolate ganache before being dipped in plain and white chocolate. They come in boxes of twelve.

All the fruit used grows wild in the hedgerows on the family farm at Sproxton and is hand-picked to ensure the highest quality. The fruits are then steeped in the spirit for four months, following the traditional method to ensure that the natural colour and flavour of the fruit is preserved. No artificial colours or preservatives are used.

Rachel supplies shops, pubs, hotels and shoots across the county and attends food fairs and country events in person so that she can talk to her customer base direct. Her show stand is made up of hedgerow products to complement her drinks. Rachel prides herself on integrating her business with the local community, having commissioned a local artist to produce the label designs and hiring local young mums to do the fruit picking. In 2005 she won the 'Young Entrepreneur of the Year' award at the CLA Game Fair and in 2008 reached the finals of the Waitrose Small Producer Awards.

**Melton Mowbray Hedgerow**
**Liqueurs**
Beech Tree Farm
21 Main Street
Sproxton           **Tel:**      01476 861058
Leicestershire     **Email:**    info@meltondrinks.co.uk
LE14 4QS           **Website:** www.meltondrinks.co.uk

## SWITHLAND SPRING WATER

In 1998 farmer Brian Beeb called in a hydrogeologist to see if the spring water on his land had any commercial value. A 300ft deep bore was sunk to reach the pure water reserve deep in the bedrock and the pure liquid gushed out. A bottling plant and warehouse has now been built on the site where 150,000 litres of spring water are bottled every week by the fifteen staff. There is also an on-site laboratory where daily checks are carried out to ensure the purity and standard of the water.

The vast bulk of the water from Swithland Spring goes to water coolers in offices, schools, factories and the like. Over 2,000 such premises are currently supplied, with some domestic business in the area around the farm.

The Swithland Spring draws water from deep beneath the Charnwood Hills. It is a moderately mineralised water that has its own unique and pleasant flavour delicately filtered by nature. The catchment area for the water that filters down to rest under the Charnwood hills is predominately woodland and parkland and still retains the unspoilt beauty of the ancient forest.

A bottling plant and warehouse has been established at the spring source in Swithland, with all the latest equipment on-site to ensure that every attention is given to cleanliness. This ensures the high quality of the water is maintained and that it is bottled in its purest form.

**Swithland Spring
Water**
Hall Farm
Swithland             **Tel:**      01509 891189
Leicestershire      **Email:**    sales@swithlandspringwater.co.uk
LE12 8TQ           **Website:** www.swithlandspringwater.co.uk

## THE DOW BRIDGE BREWERY

3 Rugby Rd
Catthorpe
Leicestershire
LE17 6DA         **Tel:**      01788 869121

## EVERARDS BREWERY LTD

Without doubt the largest and most important brewers in Leicestershire, Everards are also the oldest of the companies brewing quality ale in the county. The brewery owns dozens of pubs in the county, and supplies dozens more. Everards produces a fine range of ales, including the famous Tiger, Original and Beacon. It has won numerous awards – for its innovative advertising campaigns as well as for its excellent beers.

The Everard family has been living in Leicestershire since before the Norman Conquest, but they did not rise to prominence until the 1510s when farmer William Everard of Shenton bought his own farm and founded the dynasty of yeoman farmers. The family remained prosperous farmers in an unostentatious fashion until 1849 when William Everard founded a brewery in Southgate Street, Leicester, using local malt supplied by Thomas Hull. William ran the business for forty years, buying up pubs, opening a new brewery and generally establishing the business as a major employer. He also played a full and active role in local civic society, setting a precedent for later generations who have served as civic leaders, MPs and soldiers. In 1920 Everards bought Saison's wine and spirit business, expanding their range of goods to include almost everything that a pub could want. After the Second World War the company expanded steadily as it put emphasis on making its pubs welcoming to women and children as well as to the traditional male customer base. Then, in 1972, Tiger Special was launched. The new beer rapidly came to symbolise Everards and was soon being supplied to pubs across the country. In 1985 a new brewery was established at Castle Acres, and the firm's continuing success has seen it expanded twice since then.

Since it was founded, Everards has been a key feature of the county, and with a sixth generation of the family now involved with the business, it looks set to continue well into the future as an independent, family-based business. Among the beers currently brewed by Evarards are:

Tiger 4.2% ABV. A true award winning best bitter with universal appeal. Tiger Best Bitter is a classic example of getting the perfect balance between sweetness and bitterness. Crystal malt gives the beer its rounded toffee character.

Beacon 3.8% ABV. The hoppiness is what makes Beacon stand out.

Original 5.2% ABV. Everards premium ale and winner of the gold medal in the International Brewing Awards. Original is best known for its smooth, full-bodied taste.

Sunchaser 4.0% ABV. This is a thirst-quenching beer made in the style of a continental lager. It has subtle fruit flavours and a little sweetness within.

In January: Forty-bob 3.5% ABV. A full bodied, rich chestnut brown coloured, classic ale. Brewed with Maris Otter malt, to give a smooth malty richness, and hopped with Goldings and Northdown hops, that give the beer a peppery, spicy flavour and a delicate floral hop aroma.

In February: Pitch Black 4.3% ABV. A cask conditioned stout, Pitch Black delivers roasted malt and dark, bitter tastes.

In March and April: Sly Fox 4.0% ABV. Sly Fox is light and refreshing with a cunning hint of ginger.

In June to August: Hazy Daze 4.3% ABV. Hazy Daze is a unique offering from Everards Brewery - a cask conditioned wheat beer which is brewed with champagne yeast. The result is a great tasting ale with zesty, orange flavours and cloudy appearance.

In August to October: Equinox 4.2% ABV. Equinox returns with a new look, lower ABV and the same great taste! One of our favourite seasonal beers, Equinox is smooth and easy to drink. Its autumnal name is matched by the mature fruit flavours associated with the season.

For Christmas: Sleighbell 4.5% ABV. The best selling of all the brewery's seasonal ales is brewed to reflect the festive time of year. A rich, ruby, comforting ale full of the tastes of Christmas.

**Everards Brewery Ltd**
Castle Acres
Everard Way
Narborough          **Tel:**      0116 2014100
Leicestershire      **Email:**    mail@everards.co.uk
LE19 1BY            **Website:**  www.everards.co.uk/about

## BEES BREWERY

Bees Brewery regularly produces Navigator Bitter, Wobble and Amber Beer.

**Bee's Brewery**
1487 Melton Rd
Queniborough
Leicestershire
LE7 3FP                    **Tel:**      0116 2607715

## WICKED HATHERN BREWERY

**Wicked Hathern
Brewery Ltd**
The Willows
46 Derby Rd
Hathern
Leicestershire
LE12 5LD                   **Tel:**      01509 842364

## BARROWDEN BREWING CO.

This small pub-based brewery produces three regular beers: Beech, Hop Gun and Attitude 2. The occasional special brew is also produced.

**The Exeter Arms**
28 Main Street
Barrowden
Rutland
LE15 8WQ                   **Tel:**      01572 747247

## THE LANGTON BREWERY

This small brewery produces a range of beers for both cask-conditioned and bottle-conditioned versions. In 2008 these beers were: Wide Mouth Frog, Smalley's Stout, Mad Cow, Arapaho and Copernicus.

**Bells Brewery**
The Workshop
Lutterworth Road
Ullesthorpe
Leicestershire
LE17 5DR                   **Tel:**      01455 209940

## DOWBRIDGE BREWERY

This brewery produces four ales: Acris Bitter, Bonum Mild, Ratae'd Bitter and Fosse Ale.

3 Rugby Road,
Catthorpe
Leicestershire
LE17 6DA          **Tel:**          01788 869121

## THE DAVIS BREWING COMPANY LTD

This brewery produces an impressive range of regular beers, including: Rutland Panther Mild, Triple B, Ten Fifty, Rutland Beast and Winter Nip. They also usually produce Springtime in the spring, Gold in the summer and the highly regarded Three Kings in time for Christmas. Some of these ales are available bottled.

**The Grainstore Brewery**
 Station Approach
Oakham,
Rutland
LE15 6RE          **Tel:**          01572 770065

## HOSKINS BROTHERS

This producer has am impressive output, which includes: HOB Mild, HOB Bitter, Brigadier, Little Matty, White Dolphin Wheat Beer and EXS Strong Bitter.

**The Ale Wagon**
27 Rutland Street
Leicester
LE1 1RE          **Tel:**          0116 2623330

## THE PARISH BREWERY

The Parish produces: Parish Mild, Parish Special Bitter (PSB), Burrough Bitter, Farm Gold and Baz's Bonce Blower. Some of these beers are also available in bottles.

6 Main Street
Burrough-On-The-Hill
Leicestershire
LE14 2JQ          **Tel:**          01664 454801

This brewery sells some of its beers into the Wetherspoon chain, which is an impressive feat that reflects well on the quality of the beers which include several with a canal-themed name. The beers regularly produced include: Chancellor's Revenge, Kiln House Bitter, Cavendish Bridge, Cavendish Dark, Cavendish Gold, Reverend Eaton, Whistle Stop, Narrowboat and Five Bells.

**Shardlow Brewing Co Ltd**
The Old Brewery Stables
British Waterways Yard
Cavendish Bridge
Leicestershire
LE72 2HL           **Tel:**       01332 799188

The Steamin' Billy Brewing Company was founded in 1995 and named after a Jack Russell dog owned by the landlady of the Cow & Plough. All the subsequent ales had some link to the dog, who featured in the artwork on the beer logos. Barry Lount and Bill Allingham began brewing beers to supply the Cow & Plough and the Vaults in Leicester. Before long the fledgling company was leasing another pub, this time in Norfolk – the Robert Catesby, a sixteenth-century inn. The fourth outlet was found, this time back in Leicestershire, when the former parcel offices at the railway station were turned into a real ale bar. In 2003 Billy & Barry expanded the Steamin' Billy brand opening their fifth venture: The Paget in Loughborough. This was followed by The Western in Leicester in November 2007.

Steamin' Billy produces the following ales:

**Billy's Strong Bitter** 4.7% ABV. A full-bodied beer which exhibits a hint of golding hops, its unique character produces a good, honest, hoppy aftertaste which is dangerously drinkable.

**Steamin' Billy** 4.3% ABV. Based on the Golding Hop it's lightly pronounced floral flavour/aroma is derived from dry hopping with Golding hops, which really show through on drinking. A well-rounded beer with a satisfying aftertaste.

**Billy's Blast Off** 5.3% ABV. Dark ruddle in colour, strong but balanced, originally brewed for Leicester Beer Festival 2004.

**Fox's Revenge** 7% ABV. Voted Best Beer at CAMRA's Leicester Beer Festival 2003.

**Grand Prix** 3.6% ABV. Traditional dark mild with a hint of fruit and chocolate complimenting a roasted bitter finish, a full flavoured mild. A winner with mild drinkers.

**Howlerween** 4.5% ABV. This autumnal beer is copper coloured giving it a warming appearance, but with a strong floral flavour.

**Knock Out** 7.1% ABV. Billy's version of the winter nip, slightly sweet dark and dangerously delicious.

**Lazy Summer** 4.4% ABV. Both Goldings and Saaz hops are used in this most refreshing golden brew, a seasonal bitter finely balanced with a subtle floral aroma, belying its strength.

**Merry Christmas** 4.4% ABV. This Christmas ale is ruby in colour, giving a rich body. Medium strength, the goldings hops again comes gently through.

**Scrum Down** 3.9% ABV. A refreshing, dark, well balanced mild whose chocolaty fruity flavours complement it's roasted bitter finish, with a hint of Golding hops coming through.

**Skydiver** 5% ABV. A strong, rich, mahogany coloured beer, the malty sweetness of which coupled with its pronounced hoppy bitterness produces a moreish and extremely drinkable pint.

**Billy's Last Bark** 3.8% ABV. The original Jack Russell, Steamin' Billy, passed away in January 2007 in his seventeenth year. This beer was issued as a mark of respect.

**Steamin' Billy Brewing Company**
5 The Oval
Oadby          **Tel:**      0116 2712616 or 0116 2720852
Leicestershire **Email:**    enquiries@steamin-billy.co.uk
LE2 5JB        **Website:**  www.steamin-billy.co.uk/

## WELLAND VALLEY VINEYARDS

Welland Valley Vineyard is a two acre English vineyard established in 1991 on a sheltered south facing slope about three miles south-west of Market Harborough. Many different French and German vine varieties are grown. The soil is loam over Jurassic clay.

The vineyard produces a variety of award-winning estate bottled wines, including white, red, rose and bottle fermented Quality Sparkling. A small volume of cider is also made on-site from traditional cider apples grown in the vineyard. Welland Valley welcomes group visits with tastings. Phone for details. Visits and wine sales from the vineyard are by prior appointment only.

**Welland Valley Vineyard**
Vine Lodge,
Hothorpe Rd,
Marston Trussell,  **Tel:**      01858434591
Leicestershire     **Email:**    welland@tiscali.co.uk
LE16 9TX           **Website:**  www.welland-vineyard.com

## CHEVEALSWARDE VINEYARDS

The name Chevelswarde is of Old English origin meaning the clearing in a forest farmed by a man named Cyfel – interestingly, a Welsh name.

The one-acre vineyard, on a south-east facing slope in South Kilworth, was started in 1973. The main planting is of Mueller-Thurgau vines, though there are also two rows of Madeleine Angevine. Mueller is much grown in the Rhine and Mosel vineyards and produces a wine of good flavour. Unfortunately it is rather disease prone, whereas Madeleine Angevine is a more reliable cropper and it too can produce wines of very good flavour. The vines are grown organically in compost-fed soil by methods approved by the Soil Association. No chemical fertilizers, complex chemical herbicides, systemic pesticides or fungicides are used and so the system is environmentally friendly.

The bulk of wine production is classed as dry, though some is more a medium–dry. Up to 1,300 bottles are produced each year. Chevelswarde has won several awards, including 'Commended' at the Mercian Vineyards Association Annual Wine Competition on three occasions.

There is also a farm shop on the site selling a wide range of organic products such as fruit, vegetables, free range organic eggs, organic breads of various sorts, milk, fruit juices, dried fruits, cereals, pizza bases, flour, sauces, olive oil, tea, coffee, tinned and bottled goods, and also a variety of Ecover cleaning products.

Chevel House
The Belt
South Kilworth        **Tel:**      01858 575309
Leicester             **Email:**    organics@chevelswardeorganics.co.uk
LE17 6DX              **Website:** www.chevelswardeorganics.co.uk

# Snack Foods

## WALKERS CRISPS

Far and away the largest food company in Leicestershire is Walkers Crisps. The company began in the 1880s when Henry Walker moved from Mansfield to Leicester to take over an established butcher's shop in the high street. The business continued as a conventional butcher's shop until 1947 when meat rationing after the Second World War began to cause problems. The company looked at alternatives to make use of the workforce and workshop space that was then standing idle. With potato crisps being increasingly popular with the public, the then managing director R.E. Gerrard helped the company shift focus and began hand-slicing and frying potatoes. In the early days the crisps were cooked in an ordinary fish and chip fryer but as the years have progressed the company outgrew such modest beginnings and began using ever larger frying machinery. The company uses only British potatoes, and some sources have been with the company since the 1950s and have seen three generations of farmers supplying Walkers.

Walkers is now owned by the holding company Frito-Lay, which in turn is a subsidiary of Pepsi. Although it is now owned by a US parent company, Walker's maintains its Leicester base and is committed to the county community. The company sponsors Leicester City football club – even the stadium is named for the company.

Famously the public face of Walker's is Gary Lineker, formerly a Leicester City footballer and England captain. He has been working with Walkers for more than ten years and has starred in over seventy adverts.

The company now employs over 4,000 people and an estimated 11 million people consume Walker's products on a regular basis. Several of what are now Walker's products were formerly well known as being produced by the Smiths or Tudors snack food companies, but these have been acquired by Pepsi and the snacks are now marketed using the Walkers logo.

The full range of Walkers' products varies considerably from month to month, but generally includes the following crisp flavours: BBQ Rib, Cheese & Onion, Chilli & Lemon, Marmite,

Pickled Onion, Prawn Cocktail, Ready Salted, Roast Chicken, Salt & Vinegar, Smoky Bacon, Steak & Onion, Tomato Ketchup and Worcester Sauce.

Other products sold under the Walkers name include: Baked Doritos, Frazzles, Monster Munch, Potato Heads, Quavers, Salt 'n' Shake, Sensations, Squares, Sunbites, Walkers Lights, Walkers Max and Wotsits.

**Walkers Snack Foods Ltd**
11 Bursom Rd
Beaumont Leys
Leicestershire
LE4 1BS          **Website:** www.walkers.co.uk

# Bakers

## THE BRUCCIANI BAKERY

Pride of place in the Brucciani product range goes to the breads. From humble cobs to ciabatta, Brucciani produce a wide range of breads for cafes, for sandwiches and for customers. They also make a range of sandwiches ranging from traditional cheese & onion cobs to chicken tikka ciabattas. The company also makes pastries in a bewildering range of styles, both sweet and savoury. The bakery's cakes include carrot cake, chocolate fudge brownies, lemon splits, Bath buns, fancy tarts and a whole range of cream cakes. Special cakes are made to order.

**Brucciani (Midlands) Ltd**
5 Fox Lane          **Tel:**      0116 2519232
Leicester          **Email:**   info@brucciani.co.uk
LE1 1WT          **Website:** www.brucciani.co.uk

## SHAZMINF HALLA PIES

**Shazminf Halla Pies**
12 Gopsall Street
Leicester
LE2 0DL          **Tel:**      0116 2530058

## BLACKFRIARS BAKERY

Founded in the early 1980s, Blackfriars Bakery was one of the vanguard leading the way in the production of healthy vegetarian snacks. In 1988 the company decided to specialise in the production of health bars resulting in the launch of the now famous oat-based flapjack. By the early 1990s, Blackfriars had introduced an unprecedented twenty-plus new flavours, increasing product popularity to become one of the first companies to establish UK wide sales of flapjacks.

Blackfriars led the way, through research and innovation, in extending the shelf-life of flapjacks, firstly to three, and then to six months. This made the bakery's products ideal for small retail and snack bar outlets lacking refrigerated display space.

Blackfriars has recently launched the new range of Monster Muffins to complement their flapjacks. Products are available at a wide range of retail outlets.

**Blackfriars Bakery Ltd.**

| | | |
|---|---|---|
| 7-9 Blackfriars Street, | **Tel:** | 0116 262 2836 |
| Leicester | **Email:** | sales@blackfriarsbakery.co.uk |
| LE3 5DJ | **Website:** | www.@blackfriarsbakery.co.uk |

## POSH BAKES

Posh Bakes was formed in July 2003 to supply an exciting range of high quality cookies and tray bake squares. The range focuses on reduced fat products, many suitable for vegetarians, and cake products using fructose as a sugar agent. This makes the cakes ideal treats as part of a calorie controlled diet. Personalised products are produced for hotels and restaurants or to other business outlets. Products can also be produced to order for special events.

**Posh Bakes**

| | | |
|---|---|---|
| 193 Melton Rd | | |
| Leicester | **Tel:** | 01162610264 |
| Leicestershire | **Email:** | sales@poshbakes.co.uk |
| LE4 6QT | **Website:** | www.poshbakes.co.uk |

## MAYUR FOODS

Founded in 1990 in Leicester by Laxman Pankhania, Mayur Foods is still a family owned and run business. Many of the expert Indian chefs and skilled production staff have grown up with the business, staying in the company from leaving school to the present day.

Originally, the company built its reputation on a range of traditional naans, chappatis, pittas and tortillas – Indian breads made to Indian recipes by an Indian company. These breads were baked in traditional, authentic Tandoor ovens, which allowed the production of restaurant quality, hand-crafted products for the retail trade. The company still produces this full range of traditional breads, but is now moving forward to produce a range of other baked goods. These include hermetically sealed naans for the general grocery market outside of Leicestershire and an innovative range of pre-filled Peshwari breads.

**Mayur Foods Ltd**

| | | |
|---|---|---|
| 4 Dryden Street | **Tel:** | 0116 2620720 |
| Leicester | **E-mail:** | sales@mayurfoods.com |
| LE1 3QE | **Website:** | www.mayurfoods.com |

Leicester Bakery Limited has been baking speciality breads such as pitta and naan for twenty-two years and has grown to become one of the largest such companies in the UK. The company now distributes all over the UK and to several countries in Europe. The business now has three modern fully automated production lines and employs twenty-five people. Despite this it remains a family owned business.

**Leicester Bakery Limited**
Sabat Building
Kent Street          **Tel:**       0116 2539790
Leicester            **Email:**     info@leicesterbakery.co.uk
LE2 0AY              **Website:**   www.leicesterbakery.co.uk

Other titles published by The History Press

## The Workhouse Cookbook
PETER HIGGINBOTHAM

Containing a complete facsimile of the 1901 Manual of Workhouse Cookery, the recipe book that every workhouse chef turned to when making gruel, this book will fascinate chefs and historians alike. Richly illustrated with more than 100 photographs, it covers all aspects of life and food in the workhouse. With sections on how to brew the perfect workhouse cup of tea and the menu for a typical workhouse Christmas dinner, this is a unique, shocking, evocative exploration of food in a system that has now gone for good.

978 0 7524 4730 8

## Bread: A Slice of History
JOHN MARCHANT, BRYAN REUBEN & JOAN ALCOCK

Whether you like your bread white, sliced and wrapped or stone-ground and wholemeal, or in the form of baguettes, bagels or brioches, this book will tell you how they evolved and the technological, social and economic changes that brought them to your local baker or supermarket at a price you can afford. The past 130 years, in particular, have seen dramatic changes in the way bread is made and in the patterns of consumption. Here is an authoritative overview of the most important of foodstuffs.

978 0 7524 4748 3

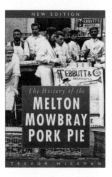

## The History of the Melton Mowbray Pork Pie
TREVOR HICKMAN

Trevor Hickman is without doubt the greatest expert on the history and development of the Melton Mowbray pork pie, and this lavishly illustrated book is a fascinating record of the people and places associated with the origins, development and production of this famous foodstuff. For this new edition the text has been completely updated and almost thirty previously unpublished photographs have been added.

978 0 7509 4324 6

## Leicestershire Events: A Pictorial History
BRIAN A ELLIOTT

Leicestershire has had an eventful history. As with other counties, for the most part the story is of the centuries-long progression of the agricultural years, the growth of towns, of industry and of population. But, from time to time, something happens that, if there had been television, would have put Leicestershire on the news and in the headlines of the next day's papers. For those who now live in the county, there is an enormous fascination in knowing what happened next door, down the street, or in the next hamlet, in the past.

978 1 8607 7280 1

Visit our website and discover thousands of other History Press books.

**www.thehistorypress.co.uk**